TOUCHSTONES

TOUCHSTONES

Spiritual Awakenings in Everyday Life

By

R. SCOTT COLGLAZIER

Chalice Press
St. Louis, Missouri

Biblical quotations, unless otherwise noted, are from the *New Revised Standard Version Bible*, copyright 1989, Division of Christian Education of the National Council of Churches of Christ in the USA. Used by permission.

Cover: Michael Domínguez
Art direction: Michael Domínguez
Interior design: Wynn Younker
Cover photo: © Corbis/George Huey (Image 63909)

This book is printed on acid-free, recycled paper.

Visit Chalice Press on the World Wide Web at
www.chalicepress.com

10 9 8 7 6 5 4 3 2 1   99 00 01 02 03 04

Library of Congress Cataloging–in–Publication Data

(Pending)

Printed in the United States of America

Table of Contents

Introduction

It's the day after Christmas, and I'm exhausted. Maybe that's the hazard of being a minister. Speaking at three Christmas Eve services has left me empty and dark. It's one thing to talk to hundreds of people about Christmas angels; it's completely another to find one for yourself.

I can't seem to find one anywhere.

I've made my way to Brown County, Indiana, something of an artists' colony and tourist village, and here I start a fire in an old stone fireplace. I like the stones, how they look, how they feel when I rub my fingers across them. I'm waiting for friends to arrive later in the day.

In the fall, people from all over the Midwest come here just to see the colors of leaves splashed against the landscape of gently rolling hills. This place is beautiful, and I could live here forever. Years ago artists such as T. C. Steele went to Paris to learn how to paint. Most artists have to go to Paris eventually; it's a right of passage. But it's here, back to these Indiana hills, these towns named Gnaw Bone and Bean Blossom, that they return to swirl brilliant oils upon their canvases.

But today, in midwinter, few people are here. Little color. Three inches of snow cushions the ground, and more is falling from the gray sky. Winter in Indiana is stark and forlorn.

In the afternoon I read a book of poetry, a new one by Mary Oliver, and tend the fire. I like the artistry of a fire. The solitary ritual of getting the logs, knocking the snow off, poking the hot logs so that they burn evenly, and then watching the flames dance to an unknown music. Nothing is better than a fire and a glass of wine.

Late in the afternoon my mood quickly changes. Friends have traveled several miles to see my wife and me, have dinner, drink wine, and share the gift of friendship. These aren't just good friends; these are the best of friends. Years ago an electrified Walt Whitman wrote, "To press the

1

flesh with my friends is enough." And well it should be! Jerry and Diane have been friends now for almost fifteen years.

We have gone through marriages and children and sick parents together. When work became too much for any of us, we could pick up a phone and know that the other would listen, both empathetically and critically. A rare combination! We were in school together and have watched each other, one by one, move past our formal education to the larger and appreciably more difficult task of composing a life. We assume each other like facts, vital parts of a mystical mathematical equation. We've gone through the women's movement, the men's movement, the New Age movement. We've had midlife crises, professional crises, personal crises. Stream after stream we've jumped in and tested the waters, but we've always been there for each other when we've climbed out and tried to dry ourselves off.

I'll never forget the first time I went to California and participated in a workshop at the Esalen Institute. Jerry and Diane picked me up at the airport, and all I could do was talk giddily about "all these new ideas, all these new people, all these new methods, and to top it all off," I explained with the enchantment of a child, "I soaked in a hot tub every day!"

William Blake said it well: "Exuberance is beauty."

Ah, we have been beautiful together!

I hear their car pull up to our little Indiana house, and I jump up and say to my wife, "They're here!" I give the fire another poke on my way to the door and watch sparks fly up the dark chimney. I'm already feeling better.

During the afternoon, we peel back the onion layers of conversation.

"How are things going?"

"Fine."

"How are the kids?"

"They're doing great."

"And yours?"

"Oh, wonderful. Just great. Here are some pictures."

I notice the icicles hanging from the eaves outside the window. In the dim light they look stately, like they could last forever. Nothing lasts forever, I know, but I think there is something enduring about friendship, some lasting quality that I want to believe in tonight. There are a few of those folks like that for us. Jerry and Diane. Ron and Leslie. Dale and Cheryl. Chris and Lisa. But not many.

"How's your mother?"

"Better."

"Tell us about your new house."

"Oh, it looks just like a Victorian cottage…"

Diane loves to describe. She loves the sensuous feeling of describing the perfect window, the slant of a roof, the perennial garden that holds forth so much promise toward the warmth of spring's arrival. And we let her go on—not that we could stop her. But she goes on, and we delight in her descriptions.

And so it goes. Layer after thin layer, peeled back, examined, discarded. Repeated again and again and again. Until dinner. Dinner becomes a feast of conversation. Wine, beer, and pizza. Mysteriously, we move past the social graces of couplehood and begin arguing about some movie, some book, some new idea with which one of us has been toying. I believe arguing is a sacrament for us. Each of us, intense in his or her own way, flexes opinions like shiny muscles in Gold's Gym. Someone reads a poem. Someone relates a menacing dream. One of us recently visited a clairvoyant and got a "reading." How's that for interesting?

But off it goes. Conversation moving like a roller coaster, flying up and down like little cars on a track, defying gravity, thumbing its nose at inertia, looping round and round and round, diving downward, careening upward, hands up in the air, screaming. And in all the movements of our conversation we hold on to something sacred for ourselves and one another.

Sometime during dinner, I'm not sure of the exact moment, but at one of those lulls when we catch our breath before going around another turn, I look at them and feel something so human, so alive, that all I can say is, "You know what we've become, don't you? We're *touchstones* for each other. That's it. We're *touchstones.*"

In medieval times the touchstone was used as a measurement to determine the weight of gold. The gold, measured against the weight of the touchstone, held forth the promise of life, of future, of opportunity. The touchstone provided an indication for well-being, prosperity, even life itself. Touchstones functioned as criteria for what is precious. What *is* precious?

In the second century, a theologian named Irenaeus said, "The greatest glory to God is a human being fully alive." Yes, aliveness! Aliveness is what is most precious; it's the gold of contemporary life. And we want it. We all want it. We're hungry for it like food, thirsty for it like water. In fact, some of us even become addicted or wounded or exhausted just looking for it. We crawl through the desert, hide in the attic, cry through the night, all because we want to be alive.

Somehow we know, instinctively, down in the depth of our souls, that the enemy we face is not death, but deadness. Not extinction, but the extinguishment of some original life zest. The battle each day, for most of us at least, is not physical survival as we try to do a good job at work, pay bills while sitting in our kitchen, or sit in traffic waiting for the light to turn green. Physical survival, in some ways, is easier now than at any other time in the history of civilization. Yet, there is some lust for living, the elusive *elan vital*, that is beyond mere survival. If it's lost or misplaced or buried, our living and the living of those around us become unbearable. A generative energy wants to live, thrive, display itself like the feathers of a peacock. It's no small moment in Dante's *Inferno* when the center of hell is discovered to be a frozen wasteland. Hell is when life freezes and there's no flow.

Coming to life is everything.

The poet Rainer Maria Rilke invites the feeling of life energy in many of his poems. But perhaps no poem is more insightful than when he mentions living life in "growing orbits." The orbiting of Rilke is not the futility found, for example, in the myth of Sisyphus. This circling is intentional, moving in orbit after orbit in search of some place in the universe. It's not futility that Rilke captures but exuberance.[1]

How do I live in growing orbits? And how do I become fully alive, super-alive to the gift of my life? How do I quit playing games with my life potential, truly being present with the gift of each hour, each day of my existence on this earth? How do I wake up to joy? Ecstasy? Intimacy? Meaning?

One answer is the word—*touchstones*. We need touchstones in our lives, those moments of experience when we rediscover our life essence, regain our bearings, remember where we've been, and gain insight about where we're going. Touchstones become maps for the soul. We become soulmates with Columbus, Magellan, Balboa, using touchstones for the adventure of sailing upon uncharted waters. There is some river of life that we must all find. Some Eden that invites our playfulness. We become cartographers of our own souls. Touchstones become signs, experiences that guide us when we find ourselves in the midst of storms. Better yet, they occasionally lead us to the calm eye of the storm.

Two ideas that I believe to be true:

1. Life longs to journey toward life, not toward an inevitable demise to death, but to greater and greater experience of living.

2. Living the journey requires touchstones, moments that break open to us vitality and spiritual awareness.

What I observe, as well as experience at a personal level, is that touchstones are becoming harder and harder to find, precisely at a time when they are needed more and more in our culture. Surf the chat rooms of the Internet and what you find are amorphous personalities searching for someplace to dock their boats in cyberspace, hungry for some connection that sufficiently matters. People type in their sex life, their fantasy life, their career life. Faceless code names hop from one on-line conversation to another the way bees buzz flowers as they try to make ultimate honey. People long for a real sense of place, of name, of being known and knowing. The proverbial Archimedes point has proven itself more elusive at the end of the twentieth century than at any other time in history. Essential to the human experience is the need to touch the texture and fabric of meaningful experience—something hard, something soft, something rough like the bark of a maple tree—but a connection with texture, as close and as real as our fingernails. Touchstones.

Chris is a good friend of mine. He's one of the few people in my life on whom I can count to push me, who expects more of me than what I would normally like to give. He lives out there on the edge with a courageous and adventurous spirit and usually is saying to me in one way or another, "Come on. Let's go. There's room on the edge for one more."

Several years ago he and I were serving as counselors at a youth camp. This particular afternoon we had gone for a run on some country roads. While we were running we found an old railroad track stretching between two large hills. I should probably tell you that I'm scared of heights and dread the exposed feeling I have when I'm high in the air. It's a fear which, although not paralyzing, I try to avoid as much as possible.

Chris said, "Let's go up the hill and take a look at that railroad track."

We climbed up the hill and stood at the beginning of that narrow bridge. It was high. Really high. No guardrails. Just steel track and old splintered railroad ties. It looked like it was a mile to the other side. It wasn't, but it sure did look like it. I knew exactly what was coming next.

"I bet we could walk across this bridge," he said with a devilish smile on his face.

"You've got to be crazy!"

"No, really, we can do it."

"But, Chris," I said, "you don't get it. I don't want to walk across the bridge. Forget it!"

"It won't be a problem."

"Oh, yes it is. It's a big problem. I'm not going to do it."

I couldn't have been more emphatic. I wasn't ready. Not this risk. Not facing this awful fear of height that has plagued me for a lifetime. I wanted to run all right, but in the opposite direction of the bridge.

"Oh, come on. It'll be fun."

"Forget it!" I tried again to make the point as emphatically as I could.

And then he said, "I'll tell you what. I'll go first, and then you can follow and hang on to my shirt."

There wasn't a cloud in the sky. The sun beat down furiously like a big engine, and between drops of sweat I squinted my eyes and watched him take that first step across the bridge. I don't know what possessed me, but I followed. I started inching my way over the railroad ties like a slug. There I was, a thirty-five-year-old man, taking baby steps, hanging on to his shirt, and I was terrified, absolutely terrified.

I kept saying, "I don't want to be doing this. I don't want to be doing this. I hate you. I don't want to be doing this!" But I hung on to his old sweaty shirt. I took step after step.

I remember getting to a certain point on that bridge and finally giving myself permission to believe that I wasn't going to die. A discovery not to be underestimated in that situation! In fact, a few yards from the end, I actually started to feel a little confident. Bravery is heady stuff. When we arrived on the other side, I was exhilarated that I had accomplished this little feat of courage. I didn't want to do it again, but I was ecstatic that I had made it to the other side.

In many ways, touchstones do for us exactly what Chris had done for me—they help us get to the other side. They help us move on. Achieve. Accomplish what we want to accomplish in life. Without touchstones life becomes rusty, dull, the sheen of vibrancy lost. But with them, life begins vibrating with energy and life.

We are at a time in our culture when we need touchstones more than ever. Many of us are working at jobs that are increasingly stressful. Wages have fallen behind. The job market has become fiercely competitive. Companies that once promised to reward loyal workers have slashed jobs to ameliorate earnings for anxious stockholders. Companies such as AT&T lay off thousands of workers without blinking an eye. And even the high-rolling CEO—replete with high salary, stock options, and benefits—knows that it is just a matter of time before the other shoe drops and he or she is ousted. Longevity and loyalty have been replaced by free agency and hostile takeovers. The pressure in business "to get it while the getting is good" is enormous.

Families, at one time considered to be sources of recreation and rest, often have become as stressful as our jobs. In fact, one recent article in the *New York Times* suggests that people are going to work and staying there longer precisely because home has become more stressful than work. Certainly families have unprecedented opportunities to enjoy a rich and full life. Children are taken, sometimes pushed, to swim teams, tennis lessons, dance lessons, computer camps, baseball, softball, art lessons, and more. All of these represent a potential intensity of joy and fulfillment. At the same time, the stress that families are placing themselves under and the burden that many of them are experiencing are nothing less than damaging to the soul. The crunch of time, money, and sheer emotional energy for family relationships is frightening.

I'll never forget the ten-year-old girl who confessed to me one day that she "was just *burned out* with gymnastics." Imagine that, burned out at ten years of age!

If both parents are working, you can count on a frantic life pace. If the family has been split by divorce, you can count on the frantic pace plus the emotional intensity of moving back and forth between two domestic settings. It's not so much a question of morality—as some want to believe regarding changing family structures—as it is the issue of health and well-being for those living in these increasingly complex social configurations. We want so much from our families, but again and again they disappoint or, worse, embitter us. And those who are single and single is, by the way, a family unit—face immense challenges of living whole and happy lives. One man, recently divorced, confided in me one day, "It's a whole new world out there, and it ain't pretty!"

There's a story in Hebrew literature about Abraham and one of his early encounters with God. As Abraham was journeying from his homeland, he felt an intense calling from God, a sense that God was moving him to accomplish some specific purpose in the world. That's what a calling really is—a moment of life clarification or an insight into life purpose. At the moment of calling, the divine and human meet; mystery and clarity are simultaneously present.

This clarity and profundity of mystery came to Abraham and his wife, Sarah, while they were traveling in the Negeb of Egypt. In response to this divine vision, Abraham built an altar, which is a biblical way of saying that he piled a bunch of stones on top of one another and marked the spot where he had encountered the Divine. The stones declared the message: "God was here! Our lives were changed here! We vow never to forget what happened here!"

All our lives have turning points like the one experienced by Abraham and Sarah. Crucial intersections when past meets future, hope meets history. And in these moments of self-definition, when we make decisions about what kind of persons we will be, we move forward and engage the radical process of becoming human. These are meaningful moments that pop into our lives like a hot kernel of corn. The heat is turned up, and we see what it is in life that ultimately matters, perhaps discovering new purpose that means more to us than we ever imagined possible. And in those moments we are changed forever.

For some, this is the birth of a child. For others, this might be a feeling of falling in love. For still others, it is a special accomplishment that feels more like a remarkable gift than an achievement. And strangely, at those moments when mortality breathes cold wind upon us and we feel our own life slipping away or when we have said good-bye to a loved one or friend, in those ending moments is the possibility of a remarkable new beginning. It is an opportunity to see life differently.

When Abraham and Sarah marked this moment, piling stone upon stone, feeling the flinty texture of the stones in their hands, hearing the tap of stone against stone, they were touching something deep within their own souls. Alas, this is both the crisis and opportunity of our contemporary lives—to touch and be touched deeply by divine mystery and life meaning. These moments of being "ultimately concerned" (that's the definition of faith offered by Paul Tillich) become like a spiritual continental divide from which our lives find meaning in two directions—past and future.

Clearly, our lives today need such markings. Living on the landscape of our lives, doing our own travels, following our own quests, the question becomes for all of us, *What are the touchstones we need for a fully engaged, fully vibrant, fully alive life?* Although not exhaustive, this book suggests some touchstones that have the power to transform life.

I want to begin with *relationships*. Friends, family, people with whom our lives have reached meaningful intersections, these are the people who have become touchstones for us. After exploring relationships, I move into the realm of *stories*. Stories and people go together. Part of super-alive living is the listening, telling, and retelling of stories. Stories have the power to shape our lives, and although stories are becoming harder and harder to preserve, our souls need them like oxygen.

Along with stories I place *rituals*. Ritual moments are those experiences—sometimes intentionally created, sometimes surprisingly spontaneous—that constellate meaning for our lives. We need rituals to mark our journey and to show us our way as we move forward into life. Rituals take stories and bring them into experiential focus. Rituals help stories move down from our brain and get inside our chest, fill our hands, our knees, and our toes. Rituals animate the body; rituals become our altars.

One way rituals tell our meaningful stories is through *art*. All art is highly ritualistic, both the creation of it and the enjoyment of it. Through art we see life differently. New worlds are offered. Spiritual depth is created,

+ feel

which in turn creates the very essence of aliveness. One problem with art in our culture is that it has become elitist, assigned to those whom we normally think of as professional artists. Yet artists are not just those who create art for a living. In fact, each person's finding and experiencing his or her own art is crucial to the spiritual journey. Art is especially important today in light of the technological tyranny we are facing in our society.

Another touchstone in life is *praying*. I want to expand the concept of prayer to move past traditional religious images of simple pious people bowing their heads at a dinner table or kneeling in a sanctuary of worship. There are many ways of praying, and all of them can become touchstones. Prayer is expansive, not limiting. Additionally, prayer most commonly has been understood as a way of getting something from God. I want to suggest that this mail-order-catalog understanding of prayer is not what prayer is about at all. Prayer can become a touchstone for spiritual development, even to the point that all of living becomes a prayer.

The next two touchstones often are overlooked for their spiritual potential, but each has a unique contribution to the human spirit—*play* and *work*. What is the spiritual significance of play? Why do we play? When was the last time you genuinely can say that you were playful? Related to play is our sensuousness and our sexuality. This is the territory of aliveness. And what of work? Is work drudgery or adventure? How can we infuse more life and energy, even libido, into our careers and working endeavors? And most of all, how can we find that sacred balance between work and play?

Another touchstone I find important in my life, and one to which people appeal again and again, is the experience of *nature*. Why is it that we love to vacation in the Appalachian Mountains or hike through the high Sierras? What is the lure of going to the ocean and walking along the beach for hours? Why does the cabin in the woods have so much appeal, or fall leaves, or the garden in the back of the house exploding with daffodils? And why do animals, the family dog or a powerful image of an animal in film, make us feel more human? Nature has a sacredness for which we long, and although we might not be able to articulate why it's important, we know that it is. Nature is a touchstone.

Finally, I want to talk about *community*. By community I mean something different than relationships. We are in community with those with whom we may not have a personal relationship. Yet community is a touchstone. I'm in community with AIDS patients, though I know only a few people personally who are suffering with that dreaded disease. I'm in community with the homeless. I'm in community with battered children. We are part of a greater family of people—global in scope, diverse, complex—and we are connected to them by our capacity to feel empathy for fellow citizens in the world and move toward them with commitment to a mutual sense of well-being. Community is a touchstone for human aliveness.

Throughout the book I will suggest that these touchstones can sometimes be spontaneous, surprising, even shocking to the hum, hum, hum of our existence. We find these touchstones or, better said, they find us. When we need them most, miraculously, our touchstones appear. "A teacher will appear when you're ready to learn," an old Buddhist koan teaches. And the same is true of touchstones. When we need touchstones, they often appear like gold dropped into our laps out of the sky. Inexplicably, they find us. Such is what it means to live by faith. These spontaneous discoveries become moments when we lift up our heads and yell, "Eureka!" and then go on our way as children of good fortune.

Yet, behind this book is another assumption—namely, that touchstones must be sought. Even as they seek us, we must seek them. Like lovers who write heartbreaking letters in the night or who cross prairies on lonesome trains waiting for a singular kiss in some station in the middle of Montana, so we must travel and journey and search until we find the touchstones we want or need.

Finding touchstones is like living life in meaningful orbits. To create the touchstones we need in life is to be on the great journey. Touchstones define what it means to be a human being. I invite you to read on. Seek. Search. Find. Answer the invitation. Listen to the invocations of spirit that take place every day. Find the life God calls *you* to live.

Chapter 1

Relationships: The Dance with Others

What I remember about David Bobo is his smile. When I first met him he was seventy-two years old, had slicked-back silver hair and a contagious, toothy smile that could compete with former President Jimmy Carter's. He was one of the most spiritually and intellectually alive people I had ever met. Nevertheless, his unassuming nature masked his remarkable achievements. He earned a bachelor's degree and three master's degrees and then, for good measure, finished a doctoral program when he was fifty-nine years old.

He was a pastor of an inner-city Indianapolis church, and there he cared for the homeless, the confused, the impoverished. He could give a teenage mother a box of Pampers from the church pantry and then go back to his study and translate a passage from Homer. That was the kind of man he was—great depth, great compassion, great humanity.

Part of David's remarkable story was that he had been a pastor in a denomination that was extremely conservative. It was the denomination of his childhood. But through years of study and soul-searching, he had worked through the arduous passage of religious fundamentalism. His ministry, deeply thoughtful and passionate, had become an oasis in a desert of rigidity and narrowness. People from all over the city who wanted something more in their lives, some new and fresh perspective to their faith, came to his church on Sundays to hear him preach. I, too, found myself in his office one day.

"David," I asked while my eyes scanned the hundreds of books in his office. (Years later I would inherit many of those same books, a tribute to the gift of our friendship.) "Tell me, David, how did you work your way out of fundamentalism? How did you become so open with your understanding of faith?"

Looking back on it, I see that I didn't realize then how important his answer would be for my own development as a person and as a young minister. His words would change my life. He smiled like an ancient wizard. His eyes expressed something of a gentle amusement at my youthful sincerity, but there was neither a trace of impatience nor a tone of condescension in his words. Instead, he measured each word deliberately, thoughtfully, carefully. He said, "I had to make a decision that it was *all* up for grabs, that I had to put every issue of my faith on the table. I decided to be totally, 100 percent intellectually honest, and then I decided that I couldn't worry about the consequences."

I cannot begin to overstate the impact those words had on my life. My relationship with David Bobo—especially that conversation—has been a touchstone for my life. I'm defined by it. Shaped by it. Even when I heard the words move through my ears, I felt a physical rush, a sensation of excitement and freedom and terror. That relationship gave me courage to open my mind and heart to God and radically changed my whole orientation toward life. A kind of wildness was in his words—almost a dare or at least a challenge—and in those words I immediately felt a rightness to what he was saying.

I didn't even have to think about it after I left his office. My entire being was shouting, "Yes!" A complete, unconditional, unhesitating yes. What happened was that his fierce intellectual passion gave my own intellect complete permission to search and quest and question. His depth of spirit became an invitation to find my own depth, my own authenticity, so crucial to radical aliveness. But it all happened in relationship.

Windows and Mirrors of the Spirit

Relationships are intensely wonderful, interesting, complex. Not to mention maddening, boring, unsettling, comforting, exciting, fulfilling, depressing, uplifting, and always—yes, always—mysterious. We swim in them like water. We walk upon them like earth. We breathe in them like air. We devour them like food. We want relationships. We need relationships.

Yet as we dance within a variety of relationships, we often find ourselves struggling to understand how to live in them effectively. More than that, we wonder about their meaning, their wisdom, the reasons we find ourselves dancing with this particular person at this particular moment in our lives. Every relationship, even at times the briefest encounters we have with others, can become a significant window and mirror for our spiritual and psychological lives. Frequently these relationships appear in our lives not as haphazard accidents—though we might experience them in that superficial way—but as an expression of soulful wisdom that is at the heart of life itself. In these moments with others, the divine center of the universe draws near to us the way a cat curls around our ankles when it wants attention. In this way, all relationships, even the painful ones, become moments of learning and grace, and they are mysteriously capable of yielding surprise and wonder.

I've come to this conclusion from both an intellectual and experiential perspective.

At an intellectual level, I've been shaped by the work of marriage and family therapist Harville Hendrix. In his wonderful book *Getting the Love You Want: A Guide for Couples,* Hendrix argues that people eventually marry the very person who has the power to help heal them of their deepest wounds. Behind his theory is the idea that as a person emerges from childhood, certain wounds beg for healing. As is the case with all spiritual wounds—and no one leaves childhood without them—no healing comes unless the wounds are faced authentically. Escape just doesn't work. Nor does denial. Our psycho-spiritual radar begins emitting signals, attracting the spouse who will recreate the same dynamics that wounded us while we were children. In that the relationship creates similar dynamics, the opportunity for healing also is constellated again. Whether healing actually occurs depends on the degree of consciousness that is brought to the situation. But the point that Hendrix makes is unmistakable—we marry whom we marry because we need this relationship to do something for us in our spiritual development.

Hendrix's theory is summarized in the following way:

> The ultimate reason you fell in love with your mate, I am suggesting, is not that your mate was young and beautiful, had an impressive job, had a "point value" equal to yours, or had a kind disposition. You fell in love because your old brain had your partner confused with your parents! Your old brain believed that it had finally found the ideal candidate to make up for the psychological and emotional damage you experienced in childhood.[1]

Over the years I have enlarged Hendrix's ideas and have come to believe that what he understood to be true of marriage partners is also true to some degree or another with every relationship, if not every encounter of our daily lives. Typically, we are not conscious of these relationships and encounters with the same intensity as we are in a marriage relationship, but that does not mean the spiritual intensity is not present. Relationships become spiritual touchstones for us precisely because every relationship is potentially a mirror in which we can see ourselves more clearly and a window through which we can see divine healing and love coming to our lives.

In a very real way, every relationship, whether it is with a child, a spouse, or a longtime work associate, becomes an opportunity for each of us to see the world differently, to wake up to new spiritual reality, and to move forward into greater aliveness. Therefore, as we enter into the mystery of relationship, certain questions present themselves to us: What can I learn about myself by being with this person? What hidden part of my being is revealed by this person? What part of my soul needs to be in the presence of this person? What issues of awareness are created within me when I am with this person? What qualities in this person am I drawn to when in relationship with this person?

In the case of my relationship with David Bobo, he became a window through which I could see a way of living that I had not seen before. When I encountered it through him, an immediacy within me resonated authentically. Resonance is key. It is that experience of seeing other people and sensing that they are living something of who you were always destined to become. Not that you become like them or try to childishly imitate them, but that you sense the rightness of some dimension of their being and it resonates within you, thus giving you the permission and freedom to be yourself. This is why these significant people become touchstones.

As a young man who had taken a brief foray into fundamentalist Christianity, I knew it wasn't working. I knew that intellectually I couldn't keep believing in a faith that didn't make sense, that callously excluded others, oppressed womenard, denied modern sensibilities. Yet, I didn't think I had any real alternative. In David Bobo, both as a person and through his well-timed words spoken in his book-lined office, I discovered a window through which I could gaze upon a life alternative. The alternative was within me all along, but it was animated with life only when I saw it living in another. The experience of relational resonance is one of the most sacred and most inspiring experiences in human existence.

And it can happen again and again. Maybe a businessman feels his soul wandering lonely and completely out of place until he learns about an individual such as Wallace Stevens who both wrote poems and was the CEO of an insurance company. This remarkable man married within himself two disparate callings, and the unique marriage might give someone else permission and freedom to be himself. Maybe an entrepreneurial woman finds herself floundering in life until she meets Anita Roddick, who is CEO of the successful Body Shop corporation. In meeting Roddick and observing how she brings together business and environmental concerns and a commitment to indigenous peoples of the earth, the other woman finds a deep and truthful resonance. Maybe she didn't even know it existed within her until this meeting, but she now has a window through which she can see her life and business differently. In both cases, another person becomes a touchstone of life discovery, stirring the imagination to see what is possible in life.

Yet, not all relationships are windows through which we see a new possibility. Sometimes other people become truth-telling mirrors, forcing us to see ourselves for who we are and who we are not.

Several years ago I attended a professional meeting in Indianapolis. I was there with colleagues. Some I knew well, but others were new to me. We were having an engaging period of discussion. At one point in the afternoon, a professor started reading his prepared theological paper. Everything about the paper and the presentation was tight and strained. His posture jabbed his points into us like a knife. His expressions and tones were combative. Even his breathing had a stressed quality to it. Aside from the fact that his paper was long, dense, and at times hard to follow, a negative energy about the entire presentation caused me to want to curl up in a defensive position. I was feeling a storm of resistance.

When the professor finished his presentation, the moderator asked, "Are there any questions?"

Silence. Complete. Telling. Utter silence.

We were all looking down at the table and then, glancing around to see if any of the other participants were feeling as awkward, some of us cleared our throats and stalled for time to invent the appropriate response. Rather than opening up conversation, the major presentation had shut everyone down. The paper gave no room to breathe, to think, to imagine. It was a take-it-or-leave-it moment. And its tone was to a great degree insulting. After all, we had been invited to the conference because we all had a degree of competency and discernment that should be appreciated, but the presentation basically had communicated that unless we were coming from the same perspective as the author, we were wrong, if not stupid, and had better just go home.

Not usually being bashful, I ventured the first comment. I knew I was in trouble before I even finished my response. I said, "You know, I've been thinking of the paper the entire time you've been reading. Obviously you put an enormous amount of research into the paper, and I appreciate that very much, but what has bothered me is that if you accept the assumptions of the paper, everything makes sense and is tightly argued. But if you think outside the assumptions, outside the accepted arena of the paper, it just doesn't make sense to me. And for that reason I wonder if the paper is true."

You would have thought I had suggested we begin, just for the fun of it, World War III! This man absolutely exploded. He turned beet red, lurched forward in his chair, and began interrogating me like an FBI agent.

"What do you mean it's not true?"

"What do you mean assumptions?"

"What are the weaknesses of the paper? Show me evidence."

"You can't just disagree without demonstrating in empirical evidence that it's wrong!"

Needless to say, it turned into more than a little scene. I came back at him with the same intellectual ferocity that he had demonstrated toward the group. We argued for several minutes. A few others started commenting too, and they tried to help the professor understand that the tone of the paper itself might be the Achilles[1] heel of the entire presentation. For my part, I had a sickening feeling in my gut the rest of the day. But my strong visceral reaction was not directed to him; it belonged within me.

This man had become a mirror for me. While he was reading the paper, while he punched and jabbed the air with pugilistic anger, while he defended against and deflected insight, while he lived out his distinctive brand of scholarly advancement, I had this mystical experience of knowing him. And I knew him because I had seen myself over and over again exhibit this same kind of anger and defensiveness. Afraid of not being taken seriously, I took myself too seriously. Afraid of not being the star, I tried to shine too brightly. Afraid of being discounted by my peers, I strained to put them all in their place.

That afternoon, in a conference room dotted with empty coffee cups as we sat around the table and ice melted in those nondescript plastic pitchers, I saw it, recognized it, felt it. This angry, stressed-out, uptight, defensive, belligerent, intellectual bully had become for me a touchstone. In him I saw myself clearly—not all of myself, but I saw that part of me that goes into meetings ready to defend my ideas and plans, that part of me that must always be right, that part of me that must win, triumph, conquer.

And in my defense—and his—that part of me sometimes serves the world well. I don't want to undermine the use of power and persuasion any more than I would want to discount the tenacious expression of ideas. Something is energizing about the vigorous presentation and defense of ideas. At the same time, I saw firsthand how ugly being right can be, how unproductive it can be to have a tightly argued paper and an even more tightly held psychological posture toward those you're trying to convince.

Since that meeting I have thought of that man literally hundreds of times. I have thought of him when I myself have been defensive and angry. And as I've reflected about him, I have felt myself take my foot off the emotional accelerator right in the middle of committee meetings or conversations. I do it because of what I saw in him and experienced with him that day. These kinds of encounters or relationships can become mirrors for us—touchstones that teach, encourage, and correct. When we see the deep meaning of them, our aliveness is intensified.

There's little doubt in my mind that I needed this encounter. How such a synchronic moment comes together is beyond my explanation. The old theological word for it is providence. Hendrix's work suggests that our soul starts emitting radar signals, and these people show up because without them we never would move into a new level of consciousness. Yet, what I now realize is that I don't need to explain it. What I do need is to live in openness to the touchstone relationships that present themselves again and again.

In relationship with others exists this extraordinary opportunity to see ourselves more clearly and to answer an invitation to live life differently. The meeting of ourselves in relationship with others becomes a sacred meeting. Derek Walcott captures this beautifully in his poem *Love after Love* when he speaks of "greeting yourself arriving at your own door." Relationships have the potential to do this for us. There are times when we meet people and they become windows for us. We see what we could be or, perhaps, what we've always most deeply been. At other times, people become mirrors. In them we see ourselves as we really are, and confront our own reality in unforgettable style. Either way, these relationships become touchstone moments for us, an opportunity to "feast on our life."

Archetypes and Relationships

The first time I met Brother David was at the Esalen Institute in Big Sur, California. I, along with about twenty other people, was waiting for him to start a workshop on a Sunday night. For some reason, there had been a loss of electricity that evening. Therefore, the entire institute was operating with a makeshift generator.

The room we were in was dimly lit. The wood-paneled surroundings, along with the large floor pillows we sat on, helped create a strange mood of anticipation and fascination. The participants were from all over the world. Some had previously been at Esalen, something of a laboratory of human transformation. Others, like myself, were there for the first time and feeling nervous and anxious, not to mention very much from the Midwest!

The only thing I knew about Brother David Steindl-Rast was what I had read in the Esalen catalog. His description read as follows: "Benedictine monk, hermit, psychologist, and author, has lectured on five continents. He is concerned with the spiritual challenges of our time."

As I waited for the workshop to begin, I had many questions: What is a *monk* doing in a place like this? What am *I* doing in a place like this? What's a hermit? What exactly does a hermit do? If he's a hermit, why is he not in the monastery praying? These questions danced in my head as I waited in the dark.

Brother David walked into the room, and immediately a magical energy glittered from his presence. He had a lovely smile, which was coupled with his beautiful Austrian accent. He put all of us at ease with his warm and inviting welcome. I never thought of a monk as being charismatic in nature, but that is the word that best describes Brother David. That week I would spend all day and every evening with him, exploring myths and archetypes, probing the questions of spirituality and psychology. It would become a life-changing event for me.

Yet, the greatest reward would be the simple relationship I would develop with him. On Wednesday night he asked me if I would like to go to the monastery, which was located about ten miles south of Esalen, and participate in vespers. Without even thinking, I answered, "Yes," and off we went. Not only did Brother David and I head down the highway, but we also took with us three other workshop participants.

I remember the experience vividly. We drove down Highway 1 as the sun dropped down into the ocean like a time-elapsed meteor. The air was cool and warm at the same time. We drove a few miles and then pulled off the road and silently tasted the majesty and mystery of nature. At one stop, we spotted three whales hugging the shore, a mother and two calves. We watched these graceful giants migrate their way down the California coast. Where were they going? What were they doing? Were they after this deep feeling of home, of belonging to the universe, that I longed for in myself? I remember glancing over at Brother David and seeing on his face contentment and delight. And I remember thinking, *If only I could have a little bit of what he has.*

We arrived at the monastery and enjoyed a time of prayer. *Enjoy* may seem like a strange description for prayer, but it's true. The philosopher Alfred North Whitehead used the word *enjoy* to mean being fully present, fully alive, fully aware, and engaged in the experience. It was in this sense that I enjoyed praying that evening. And likewise, I enjoyed being in the presence of the other monks. I enjoyed the simplicity of the little sanctuary perched high above the ocean. I enjoyed knowing that other monks who had died in years past were buried in the courtyard and watched over our praying like angels. And, yes, I enjoyed seeing Brother David in his *other* context. For me the whole experience had a feeling of mysticism and aliveness, ripe like a plum ready to be eaten.

Before the night was over, I had made two discoveries about myself.

First of all, I knew there was a part of me attracted to the devotion and beauty of monastic life. I couldn't explain it then nor can I now. Again, like the mystery of all relationships, I don't have to explain it. The soul loves what it loves, and that's enough! Second, I knew I would never live out monastic life in the external world as a lifestyle, but through my relationship with Brother David, I could connect with this particular spiritual energy. He lives out this soulful energy on my behalf. What is all of him is only part of me, but the fact that it is only part of me does not mean it is any less significant or meaningful.

Brother David has become not only a friend to me, but also a touchstone. When I am with him, think of him, read one of his books, or hear from him in an annual Christmas letter, it helps me touch a certain part of myself that sometimes I have forgotten. Who he is awakens that part of me that wants to be fully devoted to God, that wants to search and quest after the highest spiritual qualities of life. His life represents the quieter energies of my soul.

Relationships are important to us because different people carry archetypal energy on our behalf, and when we are around them, it brings certain dimensions of our existence to life. This doesn't mean that we want to become like the other person or even should try to become like the other person. It simply means that others carry for us spiritual energies that we are invited to awaken, connect to, and, to some degree or another, incorporate into our daily lives.

In the case of Brother David, he carries for me the energy of the magus. By magus I mean magician, religious insider, spiritual guide, priest, wizard. He has access to the things of the Divine that I need and want. His life of devotion allows him to be privy to the spiritual world in a way that I am not, at least not with any consistent frequency.

But there are other archetypes. For example, there is the archetype of the warrior. By warrior I don't mean the savage or brutal thug. Instead, I'm referring to the energy of accomplishment, achievement, honor. The warrior faces the task and knows that he or she must get the job done. The warrior is powerful and courageous. The warrior often faces tremendous adversity but knows there is a commitment to a greater cause that transcends personal suffering. Warrior energy is essential for every life, but what I'm suggesting is that certain people live out the warrior archetype in such a remarkable way that it awakens and inspires our own warriors when we are around them.

It is warrior energy that motivates a salesperson to get up in the morning and go out and make sales calls. Without warrior energy the company would never grow and advance. It's warrior energy that helps a young woman finish writing her Ph.D. dissertation. It's warrior energy that causes a dad to fight tenaciously to help a teenage son get off drugs. It's warrior energy that causes an Olympic athlete to run one more mile, lift one more set of weights, train one hour longer than the rest of her competitors. And I know firsthand that it takes a lot of warrior energy to finish a book. The magus may imagine it, but the warrior always completes it.

In relationships certain people carry this large and powerful body of warrior energy. Although we may already carry some of it, when we are with them our inner reservoir of warrior energy is stirred and begins flowing through us.

My friend Wayne, for example, is a consummate warrior. He's in sales and works as hard as anyone I know. I think he invented the motto "Work hard. Play hard"—because he certainly does. He's always about the task of mapping out strategies, exploring new markets, making better deals, developing new skills. If he loses one account, he only fires up his warrior engine to go out and secure two new ones. That's how he operates. If he has ever been discouraged to the point of defeat, I've never seen it.

Now, I can make certain observations about his life. I could suggest that he needs more magus energy to develop greater spiritual and mystical sensitivities. I could suggest that he needs more lover energy to enhance all of his interpersonal relationships. Yet, those suggestions have nothing to do with my relationship with him. For me, and probably for others, too, Wayne dramatically carries warrior energy. And when I'm feeling overwhelmed or defeated or resigned to circumstances, all I need is one hour with Wayne, and I'm ready to go out and conquer the world. Wayne is a warrior touchstone for me.

As you think about your own relationships I want to enc
to begin asking the question—*What archetypal energy does t*
person radiate on my behalf?

Carol Pearson addresses this question effectively in her book *The Hero*
Within. Pearson rightly understands the hero journey as one of the most
important cross-cultural myths in human experience. Yet, she also appreciates that there are distinct archetypal potentials that can be understood
and appreciated within the framework of that myth.

She notes the reality of the *orphan.* The orphan is an expression of
archetypal energy that lives out an intense degree of fear and abandonment.
Orphans want a caretaker in relationship, often longing for an authoritative figure to rescue them from the hard realities of life. The orphan says:
"Take care of me. Give me the answers. Save me." What must be appreciated is that there is orphan in all of us. That's why most of us feel lonely at
times in our lives. But as we live upon the web of complex relationships,
certain people will live the orphan archetype with painful distinction. As
we relate to these people we have a choice—*Will we become a rescuer or a*
despiser?

But there is another opportunity. As we see the orphan so clearly, this
other person becomes a touchstone for our deeper self-understanding.
Rather than rescuing or despising the orphan, we see the orphan, and it
helps us feel our own sense of abandonment, our own woundedness, even
our personal longing for healing, help, and safety. We may not live out the
orphan archetype as intensely as some. We don't need to. Yet seeing the
orphan in others helps us to stop and feel the orphan within ourselves.
This can be a positive moment in our relationships and in our individual
spiritual development.

Pearson also distinguishes the archetype of the *martyr.* The martyr is
the one who suffers for the well-being of others. The martyr gives himself
or herself to a transcendent cause. Rather than wanting to receive the
care of others like the orphan, the martyr wants to offer care, even to the
point of personal pain and sacrifice.

It should be noted that all archetypes have positive and negative expressions. The orphan can be positive when it is expressed in the form of
recognizing genuine need and emotional receptivity in relationships. The
martyr can be positive in the form of giving to others by working in a
soup kitchen at a downtown mission or by taking a cut in salary for the
well-being of the company. But all archetypes can have a negative expression. The orphan can become so needy that a mutual relationship becomes impossible. The martyr can give to others to the point of never
recognizing his or her own legitimate emotional needs. The warrior, rather

than being a powerful leader initiating positive change in the world, can become brutal, cut off from any tender dimension of the human spirit, and divorced from reality. The magician, typified by my friend Brother David, can move with grace between the inner and outer worlds of reality to benefit others through authentic sharing and teaching. At the same time, the magus can become lost in the inner world of vision, practically hallucinating about spiritual reality and thus losing touch with important worldly reality.

Many archetypal expressions exist. I've noted only a few. I could mention the wanderer, the king, the queen, the lover, the wise old man, the crone. Each person with whom we are in relationship carries one, if not more than one, of these archetypal expressions. Our opportunity in relationships is to recognize these psychological-spiritual energy expressions, reflect on them in a way that facilitates our own growth, and appreciate the fact that we are in relationship with these people precisely because we need in one way or another the archetype they are carrying.

When I was a child my grandmother would take me on shopping trips to the big city of Louisville. Coming from a small town in southern Indiana, Louisville felt so big, so sophisticated, so full of options. After shopping downtown at Bacons department store, we would go out for lunch at the Blue Boar Cafeteria. At the Blue Boar you could order anything! To my eye it looked like there were millions of choices. Cole slaw. Cottage cheese. Tossed salad. Gelatin salad. Roast beef and chicken and fish and pork. And vegetables? Too many to name. Desserts were chocolate pie, lemon pie, coconut cream pie, chess pie. The array of choices was dizzying.

I would say, "Mammaw, may I have a dessert?"

And her answer was always the same, "Of course. This is our day to splurge!" And splurge we did. At the Blue Boar Cafeteria the world seemed so rich and full.

In many ways this is true of archetypal realities in the network of human relationships. There is so much spiritual energy to splurge on in this world. Some carry the warrior. Some carry the lover. Some carry the queen. Some carry the king. The fascination of relationships is that each person in our life becomes like an item on the Blue Boar steam table. We pick and choose, taste and digest. Some archetypal expressions, especially the shadow side of them, we'll see but want to avoid. Others we'll identify with and make room for in our own life adventure. In either case, the archetypal realities of life become for us a relational feast.

In the case of Brother David, I know I will never become a Benedictine monk. Yet, strangely, he lives out for me what I can live out only in small bits and pieces in my everyday life. With a wife, three children, and a demanding profession, I know I can make room for only brief times of study, prayer, and reflection. Yet the fact that I am in relationship with him helps me touch the priestly magus within myself. When I visit him at the monastery in Big Sur, walk those lovely grounds, or attend vespers in the evening, I know that I'm at least touching a part of my personality. I see him, but I know I'm also seeing a part of myself. That's the beauty of relationships[2] becoming touchstones. They are sacred, mystical, marvelous. No wonder the poet Rumi said, "Be grateful for whoever comes, because each has been sent as a guide from beyond."

The Divine Touch

At the heart of the universe is the divine being. From my perspective, God is more than simply a being "out there" or "up there." God names the center of the universe that is love, creativity, and transformation. What you finally name that divine being is actually not as important as acknowledging it. The divine being, the divine energy of life, is named differently in the various traditions of the world's religions—each of them succeeding and failing variously in its description of the divine. Yet what becomes of paramount importance is finally not description, but awareness of living with a spiritual center that is always in us and beyond us.

The thirteenth-century mystic Mechthild of Magdeburg spirals toward the divine with this description:

> O burning Mountain, O chosen Sun,
> 　O perfect Moon, O fathomless Well,
> O unattainable Height, O Clearness beyond measure,
> 　O Wisdom without end, O Mercy without limit,
> O Strength beyond resistance, O Crown beyond all majesty:
> 　The humblest thing you created sings your praise.[2]

How do you describe the indescribable? The divine being in the world is that which is both ultimate reality and the ground of reality itself. Both sun and moon, both mountain and ocean, both garden and desert. This is the divine being in the world.

I invite you to reflect on the connection between the divine being of the universe and your significant network of relationships. So far I've suggested that relationships are crucial to our self-understanding and development. I believe that is true. Yet I want to take it a step further now and suggest that relationships are touchstones to the divine. In relationships we see the nature of God, and, in fact, through them we experience God. Or perhaps better said, God draws near to us in the complex configurations of our relationships with others.

Several years ago I heard a wonderful rabbinic story. A rabbi said to his students, "So, my students, how can we determine the hour of the dawn, when the night ends and the day begins?"

One student eager to please the rabbi said, "When from a distance you can distinguish between a dog and a sheep."

"No," the rabbi replied, "I'm afraid that's not the answer."

A second student answered, "Rabbi, is it when you can distinguish between a fig tree and a grapevine?"

Again the rabbi replied with a gentle, "No."

"Please, tell us the answer then. When does day begin and night end?"

The rabbi gazed into the eager eyes of his students, paused for a long time, and then slowly he measured out the answer: "It is when you can look into the face of human beings and you have enough light to recognize them as your brothers and sisters. Up until then it is night, and darkness is still with us."

What do we recognize in the eyes of others? What do we see in our relationships? Do we see something wondrous and sacred? Do we see something of ultimate reality, something of the heart of the universe itself? Do we see God in the face of others? These are the touchstone questions we are invited to entertain.

In the case of both "my" Davids—David Bobo and David Steindl-Rast—in many ways so far apart in background, experience, and theological perspective, I found the essence of God in them. Their beauty and compassion, their depth of spirit and immediacy of love, their ecstatic joy and their meaningful suffering, all of that and more opened the door to experience what God is like.

Each person in our lives gives us some sliver of the divine being. Recently people have focused on the reality of angels in our world and how certain people become angels for us. I have no doubt that this is true. Angels, of course, become a metaphoric way of speaking about God's presence in this world. In a manner of speaking, David Bobo became an angel in my life, and David Steindl-Rast became an angel for me too. I saw in their faces the angelic quality of mother, father, brother, sister. And, most profoundly, I experienced in their presence the divine being.

Another way of speaking of this touchstone dimension is to focus on what therapists sometimes call the "inner child" or the "divine child" or, the expression that I prefer, the "golden child." This is language employed to describe this central quality in people to reflect the essence of God. Not only do people reflect the qualities of God, but more to the point, they carry something of the essence of God in their being. This God-essence is described as the "divine child," which lives not only in ourselves, but also in others. In the Christian tradition, this is intimately related to the Holy Spirit living within the lives of the sons and daughters of God.

One of the most alive moments in anyone's existence is when the golden child leaps to life and meets another human being with whom this inner spiritual connection is made. My inner child meets your inner child. And in that moment you can feel the playfulness, the joy, the pure spiritual delight of being with this person. People often experience this with a woman or man in the form of what we sometimes call flirting. By flirting I don't mean seduction nor do I mean inappropriate sexual behavior. I simply mean this childlike playfulness of being together. It's as if two people are secretly saying to each other, "Can you come out and play with me today?"

I felt this with David Bobo and David Steindl-Rast. Although both of them were serious scholars and ponderous thinkers, there was an incredible lightness to their being, some wisp of air flowed from them to me and brought me to life. And I have felt this so many times in my life. Men and women, old and young, people who awaken the golden child within me. When this happens, relationships transcend the mundane and soar toward spiritual experience. If we can't find God in our network of relationships, we probably will never find God.

Relationships become the ongoing creative work of God. Meister Eckhart has written, "Now God creates all things but does not stop creating. God forever creates, and forever begins to create, and creatures are always being created, and in the process of beginning to be created." In each relationship of our unfolding life the creative work of God is present and generates itself again and again. Jean Lanier has gone even a step further by suggesting, "I am emerging out of all the events of the world, out of their relationship. Is relationship God?"

Is it true that God is present in each person and that every relationship is a touchstone with the divine? I believe it is true. It must be true. Or at least as true as night becoming a glorious day.

Tending the Garden of the Other

Several years ago a friend gave me some beautiful hosta plants. Hostas are gorgeous, leafy plants possessing both a poetry and sensuality about them. They are perennials. If you plant them and give them even a modest amount of care, they will grow and can be enjoyed for several years to come.

When my friend brought the plants over to my house, he was extremely excited. I discovered that he's a hosta freak! He belongs to a national hosta society. He goes to hosta conventions. (Sounds exciting, right?) And the hostas he brought by as a gift were grown in his own yard and were perfect specimens. He knew the Latin names for each of them and handed them over to me like a mother leaving her children for the first time with a babysitter.

I was appreciative of the hostas. They were nice enough. And I certainly appreciated the fact that he would think enough of me to give them as a gift. Yet the truth was, I wasn't really in a gardening stage of life. I made sure the lawn was mowed, but that was about it in terms of lawn care. Landscaping didn't matter much to me either. After he left, I dug a few holes, stuck the hostas in the ground, and, when I thought of it, watered the plants. Throughout the summer I basically neglected the hostas. I think the dog dug up a few of them, too. For the most part they suffered from inattention and a lack of appreciation.

Years later, however, I've noticed a growing change within me when it comes to gardening. I now love to garden. And hostas are absolutely my favorites. I've also noticed that I like perennial plants better than annuals. The perennials aren't as immediately satisfying, but over the years they grow and bloom and provide a nice texture to the yard. And it's also true that perennials require a little work. You have to cut them down in the fall and mulch them in the winter. In the spring and summer, they have to be weeded and watered. But the perennials provide a lasting beauty that I've come to appreciate. In fact, I revel in the times when my friend calls and asks, "Could you use a few more hostas?"

Similarly, for relationships to lead to radical aliveness, they not only must be planted, they also must be nurtured, cultivated, and cared for in an ongoing way. Each person in our life is a garden that calls for attention. Or you might think about it like this—relationships are touchstones, but sometimes they need polishing!

Spiritual Practice of Relationships

I want to offer some practical ways of thinking about the ongoing care of relationships. In many ways, since relationships give spiritual life, the care and nurture of them become one of the most crucial spiritual practices of our lives.

The first part of relationship gardening is *forgiveness.* It would be difficult for me to overstate the importance of forgiveness in relationships. There comes a moment in every relationship when fantasy has a head-on collision with reality. We may have a boss at work whom we idealized at the beginning of our employment, but soon we see another side of his or her personality. We may have children whom we have idealized since birth, but now as they come into their adolescent years we see that they are selfish and angry and capable of being hurtful. This especially plays out in romantic relationships.

In romance we idealize the other: "She is the most beautiful woman in the world." "He is so handsome." "She is so smart." "He is so sensitive and caring."

In these idealizations our lives become intertwined with projected ideals and fantasy hopes. Inevitably, however, these idealizations begin to shake and shatter. The daily life of buying groceries, paying bills, and cleaning the apartment replaces the idealizations that first brought us together. Anger is felt. Harsh words are spoken. Moods mysteriously dominate. Tension. Hurt. Stress. These become woven into the fabric of relationships.

Yet, clearly, these breakdowns don't necessarily signal the end of the relationship. On the contrary, these disillusionments become opportunities to replace our initial relationship illusions with a new level of depth and understanding. But for the relationship to hang together, there must be the spiritual practice of forgiveness.

Forgiveness is essential for two reasons. It's essential for other people because eventually they will disappoint us. They may do something that hurts us. They may passively ignore some of our important needs. They may simply not measure up to our expectations. Clearly, it's not the case that this *might* happen. It *always* happens! Therefore, to be in relationship requires forgiveness.

Forgiveness is important for a completely different reason. Within each human being is the capacity and need to forgive others. What I often find is that my anger or hurt or bitter resentment is not really damaging the other person as much as it is damaging me. I need to forgive. I need to learn to let go. I need to practice the spiritual art of acknowledging the tension and then releasing it out of my heart, letting it flow into the very heart of the universe.

Related to forgiveness is the practice of *living in the present*. Relationships can't live in the past, nor is it helpful to leapfrog into the future. Relationships call for living in the here and now. To be present with the other person right now. To be spiritually and emotionally available to the person right now.

Think of the number of times you've gone to the emotional basement of your life, dusted off an old event from the past, pulled the pin, and then hurled it like a hand grenade at another person. It explodes all over the other person. And we know it. We want it to explode because if we can detonate the past, we don't have to deal with the present.

I'll never forget the couple I counseled several years ago. They were experiencing some relationship stress and came to see me in my office. To me it felt as if I were watching a table tennis match played with a live hand grenade.

What I'll never forget is that the woman said to the man, "But don't you forget what you did to me at the wedding!"

Well, that got my interest up. I wanted to know what happened at the wedding.

He immediately said, "Oh, please, don't start with that again." Obviously he had heard this story before.

She went on to describe how he had been late for the wedding ceremony. Now he had arrived at the church, mind you, but for some reason he had been late for the wedding. She was bitter, angry. What's amazing, though, is that this event had happened twenty-three years earlier. Twenty-three years! They were tragically stuck in the past. And in garden terms, it doesn't really matter what the garden looked like a decade ago or what the garden might look like in another decade; the key is to nurture the garden of relationship in the here and now.

Another spiritual practice that relationships call for is *responsibility*. It's so easy to blame, isn't it? How many times have we wanted to scream, or perhaps did, "It's all your fault!" Many of us never experience the radical aliveness relationships have to offer because we're so busy using the weapon of blame. If, for example, I blame my wife for all my unhappiness, I never have to face the real unhappiness within myself. If I blame my children or parents or company or friends for my pain, I don't have to deal with the pain myself. As convenient as it is to blame, blame always leads us down a dead-end street.

The couple I just mentioned were caught in a blame game. Although the unfortunate event of the man's showing up late for his wedding had happened twenty-three years earlier, the blaming was still buzzing in their relationship like a fly trapped behind a window. I see this in organizations all the time. The minister is blamed by a church member. The principal is blamed by a parent. The manager is blamed by an employee. A professor is blamed by a student. Obviously, people need to be held accountable for their actions, but blaming finally becomes an escape for taking responsibility for our own aliveness and well-being.

Blaming also works in another way. Sometimes we avoid responsibility by blaming others, but sometimes we escape responsibility by blaming ourselves. This is the self-blame game. Instead of being responsible for our feelings, we bury them. Instead of expressing our thoughts, we swallow them. Sometimes we hope they will just go away. Sometimes we try to pretend we're not hurt or angry or annoyed. Yet, in almost every case, a denied feeling only intensifies and comes out in unproductive ways later in the relationship.

It needs to be said that responsibility in relationships is hard work. Blaming is so much easier. When someone asks us, "What's wrong?" we quickly say, "Oh nothing." Or we respond to such a question with "Why do you want to know? You're never going to change!" Those responses become the familiar roads many of us walk.

But to say to a partner, for example, "When I come home and you're watching TV and you don't spend time talking to me, it makes me feel isolated and abandoned, and I begin feeling unloved by you" —whew! That's taking responsibility for a healthy relationship. The opposite of blame is responsibility.

Another quality of relationships is *inspiration*. By inspiration I mean the quality of bringing energy to other people in a positive way. William Blake once wrote, "Energy is eternal delight." And it's true. Part of what we do in relationships is bring energy, inspiration, aliveness to one another. At times this happens spontaneously; at other times we have to be intentional about the energy we bring to others.

What I have valued about my relationship with David Steindl-Rast has not been the words he has said or the ideas he has passed on to me, as much as my sharing in the delightful energy he radiates. I know people who had a personal relationship with one of the best religious thinkers of the twentieth century, Thomas Merton. They visited him at the Abbey of Gethsemani or hosted him for events in their homes. What they have said repeatedly was that they just enjoyed being around Merton. And although I never knew Merton personally, I feel certain that he had this vibrantly alive energy about him. One of my prized possessions is a photograph of Merton. He's at a party, wearing his austere black-and-white monk garb, flashing an effervescent smile, and he's playing, of all things, the bongos. I love it. It's not so much the technical quality of the photograph that I'm drawn to, but the energy of his aliveness that radiates through it.

I have come to believe that every person has an energy field surrounding his or her life. Some bring a positive energy of hope and alive-ness. Others, unfortunately, seem to suck energy from others. As we try to be responsible and nurture our relationships, it's helpful to ask questions such as: What kind of energy am I bringing to my relationships? What kind of energy do my words, my actions, my attitudes impart to others? What kind of inspiration do I need to breathe into the lives of the people I love the most? What kind of inspiration am I needing in my life? What do I need to do to make sure I find inspiration from others? These are the questions of energy and inspiration. Touchstones come to life when the spiritual practice of attention is given to them.

The Healing Touch

No conversation about relationships would be complete without addressing what all of us need in our relational life—namely, _healing_. It is true that none of us escapes childhood without some relational wounding. Furthermore, that wound follows us through adulthood and affects all of our relationships with others. Sometimes it is played out in the form of inexplicable anger or feelings of abandonment. Regardless of the symptomatic expression, these wounds must be addressed if relationships are to lead us to aliveness.

Singer, mystic, raving Irishman Van Morrison sings about living and working and playing "till we get the healing done." The healing we need in relationships is deep and spiritual. Until we let God touch us and transform our lives, we remain forever crippled as we relate to others. Finally, it is love that has the power to make us new. The spiritual energy of God comes to us, embraces us, puts its arms around us, and holds us like a mother holding a child. It is a love that is at once beyond us and in us. Pure gift. Pure grace.

Andrew Lloyd Webber's musical _Miss Saigon_ tells a poignant love story of a young Vietnamese woman and an American soldier. They pledge their love to each other, and she becomes pregnant with his child. Circumstances separate the young couple. In fact, he does not even know she has given birth to a child. They become separated by miles and years and cultures. Yet, throughout their long and difficult separation, the mother never gives up hope that this little child will someday have a better life. She endures tremendous hardship, even humiliating circumstances, but she does so out of an unrelenting commitment and devotion to the child. At the end of the play, the mother takes her own life, but not before she is sure that the boy will have a home in America with his father.

Could it be that this woman is an insightful symbol of God's love for each of us? Unrelenting. Passionately seeking our well-being. Deeply devoted to us. Could it be that at the heart of the universe is one who seeks us out, who longs for us, who desires the very best that is possible for us in life? More than coming to us, could it be that this God offers us a love that has the power to heal us of even our deepest wounds?

In our deepest experiences of life, there longs to be said by us all a resonating "yes."

Some open their hearts to this gift of divine love by way of prayer. Some use meditation. Still others find their entrance into the heart of God by way of worship. _How_ the door is opened is not nearly as important as making sure that it _is_ opened. The poet Kabir wrote centuries ago, "There is one thing in the world that satisfies, and that is a meeting with the Guest." Meeting the "Guest" is meeting the Divine. That happens through relationships, but it also happens for the benefit of relationships. When in the quiet of our lives we let go into the mystery of God, feeling ourselves accepted and beautiful and loved, perhaps only then are we ready to reach out our hand and be in relationship.

These people in our lives, stumbled upon, pursued, longed for but never found—these sacred constellations of personalities, unique psychologies, friends, spouses, lovers, colleagues—these are the sacred stones in our lives. We place them around our existence like an altar to some unknown mystery. But when we touch them, or they touch us, some beautiful ineffable thing comes close, and we are once more brought back to life.

Chapter 2

Stories: Telling Our Truth

In his marvelous book _Returning: A Spiritual Journey,_ Dan Wakefield begins with this sentence, "One balmy spring morning in Hollywood, a month or so before my forty-eighth birthday, I woke up screaming."[1]

What a wonderful sentence! It's the kind of sentence that begs for more. Explanation. Fill in the blanks. Interpretation. I want to know why he was screaming. What he was doing in Hollywood. Why spring? Why balmy? Why forty-eight? I read that sentence and I want the story—the narrative that both asks and answers questions. I want to hear some tale that makes sense of what I feel when I hear words such as _Hollywood_ or _spring_ or _screaming._

At the heart of the universe is story. But to say that is to be far too abstract and out of touch with daily experience. Better said is that story is at the heart of the human experience. The hearing and telling of stories is one of the most deeply human, most deeply spiritual, most deeply relational experiences we can ever have. And it's in this sense that stories become for us touchstones. We need them to become spiritually alive.

By story I don't mean some make-believe world or an expression of falsehood. My grandmother sometimes would say to me, "Now, don't you _story_!" And by that she meant, "Don't lie! Make sure you tell the truth." Unfortunately, her use of the word _story_ was far too jaded.

Stories aren't lies. On the contrary, stories tell the deepest truths of our lives, and if we aren't in the practice of understanding them, listening to them, and articulating them to others, chances are that we are the ones who will become living falsehoods. Stories are deeply true.

That beginning sentence of Dan Wakefield's actually places us right in the middle of a story. A successful writer, Wakefield had migrated from his hometown of Indianapolis to New York City to major in journalism at Columbia University. He was at Columbia when it was at the height of intellectual ferment. From there he moved to the glitzy world of movies and to the writing of television screenplays in Hollywood. Over the course of his lifetime, Wakefield had gone through the dark moods of psychological exploration, a tumultuous journalism ride filled with assignments and deadlines, the writing of books, relationships, more books, and the shadowy experimentation of his life called the 1960s.

Yet, now, at forty-eight years of age, a new story had started to emerge:

> I got out of bed, went into the next room, sat down on a couch, and screamed again. This was not, in other words, one of those waking nightmares left over from the sleep that is dispelled by the comforting light of day. It was, rather, a response to the reality that another morning had broken in a life I could only deal with sedated by wine, loud noise, moving images, and wired to electronic games that further distracted my fragmented attention from a growing sense of blank, nameless pain in the pit of my very being, my most essential self.... The day I woke up screaming I grabbed from among my books an old Bible I hadn't opened for nearly a quarter of a century. With a desperate instinct I turned to the Twenty-third Psalm and read it over, several times, the words and the King James cadence bringing a sense of relief and comfort, a kind of emotional balm. In the coming chaotic days and months I sometimes recited that psalm over in my mind, and it always had that calming effect, but it did not give me any sense that I suddenly believed in God again. The psalm simply seemed an isolated source of solace and calm, such as any great poem might bring.[2]

With those words I begin to hear a story. More than a sentence, a narrative begins coming together, forming pictures, feelings, impressions. I find myself not just listening to someone else, but finding myself too. Stories do that. They become touchstones for spiritual aliveness because they lend themselves to self-reflection. A man in crisis? I can relate. A middle-aged man in crisis? I can relate again. A human being searching for meaning at the end of a rope? I've been there, not once, but more than once. Again and again I have tried to listen to my life, both its longing and its satisfaction, its feeling of being lost and found. Suddenly, I listen to his story, and I hear my own story. Not as Narcissus mesmerized by the beauty of his own reflection—though at times stories help us do that too—but as one who hears within another's narrative familiar notes that become a soulful descant shared and sung together.

It Takes Two to Story

Stories become essential touchstones because they connect us with people. To hear them means we must transcend ourselves. But in the act of transcending ourselves, we touch the sacredness of transcendence. I listen to Dan Wakefield and realize that I'm not hearing the mere narration of events—A leads to B and B leads to C. Instead, I'm accepting the invitation to participate in the mystery of another human being—his pain, his desperation, his hope. We are alive only when we are willing to answer that invitation.

It is true, I think, that part of the compelling power of listening to the stories of others is that they are not slick and flat like a nonstick griddle. Instead, stories have texture, undercurrents, hidden corners, and surprise doorways. Yes, I sometimes can empathize with those who desire to live in a simpler time, to exist with simpler rules to and to cope with simpler consequences. But this is not life. Just as relationships become complex— at times overwhelmingly complex—so also do stories. Stories invite the awesome experience of mystery They invite us, sometimes demand us, to stand there with our mouths wide open, gaping in horror or amazement or both at the complexity of feelings found in the story.

Perhaps the word is resonance. I go and see movie the *Field of Dreams* and feel within me the spiritual experience of resonance. I feel connected, touched, inspired. I see Ray Kinsella build a baseball field, all because he wants to reconnect with his father, who has been dead for years, and I feel myself resonating with that story. I listen to Bruce Springsteen sing a story of young love or of working despair or of love gone bad, and I resonate with it. I read a story from the Bible about Joseph and his amazing dreams, and I find myself dreaming my own dreams again. I transcend myself long enough to hear the story of another, and in that encounter of listening, I participate in the complexity and texture and mystery of life itself.

It's not enough that I hear Dan Wakefield describe his experiences; I'm engaged by them in a soulful, participatory way. And the possibility of this sacred, beautifully human experience of being engaged in my own life happens again and again as I swim in a sea of stories. Stories define the adventure of daily living.

Think of the number of stories we hear each day. Our spouse offers an innocent childhood memory, but the moment that story is heard, really heard, it becomes a transcendent moment of sharing. A secretary confides that she and her husband are getting a divorce. That's more than information; it's an invitation, if not a human appeal, for someone to listen, to understand, to resonate. You innocently ask the teenager at McDonald's how she is doing, and to your surprise, she answers. Not with a typical adolescent grunt or even a polite "fine," but she tells you a story, a story of her car breaking down on the way to work, a story of a boyfriend breaking up with her, a story of what she and her friends are going to do after work that night. Every day is a day of stories.

This is why the touchstones of relationships and stories are so intimately related. Even as relationships can become the sacraments of the divine, so stories often function as the chalice and paten for relationships. Through the stories of our lives, relationships are built. One of the most important spiritual practices we can undertake, therefore, is the development of listening lives.

Ask yourself the following: How often do I feel myself present while listening to the story of another? Do I find myself skipping over the narratives of others so that I can speak? What new stories am I learning about people with whom I am the most familiar? What sense of surprise has the story of another brought to my life recently? What in the story of another do I find most deeply true in my own experience? These are the questions that swirl around the touchstone of stories. More than swirl, these questions open the door to magical transformation within each of us.

In You I See Me

Even though I've never met Dan Wakefield, I feel as if I'm in relationship with him. He was vulnerable enough, not to mention courageous enough, to share some of his story. Yet his story moves within me like personal wisdom. His story takes up residence within my soul, and although that is like welcoming a guest into my being, it is at the same time like coming home to myself.

I remember sitting one day in my living room and hearing the doorbell ring. I answered the door only to find total strangers standing on my front porch. They smiled and introduced themselves to me. Quickly they began a narrative of how they used to live in the house years ago, how they were passing through on vacation, and how they wanted, if I wouldn't mind, to come in and see the place again. Something was both delightful and unnerving about their request. But as I showed them through the house, telling them what we had done to it recently and listening to their stories of children and parties and remodeling projects, I could see a sense of home begin to awaken in their eyes. I could almost see the children rebuilding their stories inside their brains so that they would have them the rest of their lives.

Many times when we hear a story, it's like coming back home. Some sleeping-bear part of our spiritual life begins to awaken from slumber, and when we hear the right narrative, the familiar twist, the resonating plot line of another, we find ourselves more alive than ever before. In you I see me—and that becomes a tremendous gift of spiritual insight. Those stories are floating out there, showing up like strangers on our doorstep, angels if you will. If we will listen for them and to them, there awaits a new level of aliveness.

The spiritual life primarily has been conceived of through the metaphors of journey and home. I wouldn't dare suggest that one is more important than the other. In fact, stories are essential for both. As we journey and listen to others, we hear stories, and we find ourselves empowered to press on, face what must be faced, and never give up on the sacred calling of our becoming. Perhaps it is the story of an Abraham journeying through the Negeb of Egypt, escaping with his life, worshiping God upon crudely made altars, and making an economic fortune with uncanny consistency. I hear his story of journey, and I see myself. Or it might be an Odysseus who is far from home and faces obstacles of immense complexity. In his story, I hear my story of journey.

But home also is important. Home is that spiritual feeling of "Aha, this is it. I'm where I should be. Yes! That's me. This is who I am—really am!" These soulful exclamations that rise up within us like mysterious wind currents guiding a hot-air balloon are essential to our spiritual development. Often these gusts of the Spirit come to us when we hear the stories of others.

The story of Dan Wakefield proceeded to unfold like points on a computer graph. He faced the issue of his need for sobriety. The need for physical exercise. He moved from Hollywood back to Boston. He noticed an immediate positive impact upon his blood pressure. These are mere points on a chronological continuum. The real narrative of his spiritual life continues with a Christmas Eve story.

Just before Christmas I was sitting in The Stevens, a neighbor-hood bar on Charles Street, drinking a mug of coffee while friends sipped their beers. I didn't mind being in bars and around other people who were drinking while I was on the wagon, in fact I preferred it. I was comfortable in the atmosphere, and if I couldn't drink any booze at least I could inhale its nirvanic scents and maybe I even got a kind of "contact high" as musicians were said to do off others smoking grass. A house painter named Tony who was sitting at the table with me and some other neighbors re-marked out of the blue that he'd like to go to mass somewhere on Christmas Eve. I didn't say anything, but a thought came into my mind, as swift and unexpected as it was unfamiliar: *I'd like to do that too*...I found myself that Christmas Eve in King's Chapel, which I finally selected from the ads on the *Boston Globe* religion page because it seemed least threatening. It was Unitarian, I knew the minister slightly as a neighbor, and I assumed "Candlelight Service" meant nothing more challenging than carol singing...I looked inside and saw a beginning."[3]

If we will bear with the story long enough, hang onto it as if our life depended upon it, the miraculous just might happen. I listen to his story and find myself moving from "waking up screaming" to "I looked inside and saw a new beginning." Seeing a new beginning is what is possible in the stories we hear. I listen and can see how life could be different. I listen and feel how life could begin again. I listen and find myself coming home. I need relationships to enhance my aliveness, but I need the stories to help me see how aliveness is possible.

Finding Our Voice

The autobiographical quality of the spiritual life is undeniable. Each of us is writing a story, creating a life, becoming some poem we send out into the universe. We are novelist, poet, and playwright of our own existence. Sadly, some of us never awaken to the story we are writing. As one man told me a few years ago, "I've never thought much about my life; I've just been living." Nevertheless, conscious or unconscious, this man, as all of us, is still composing a life.

Yet, there are moments when we do think about our lives, and usu-ally these are moments when we have a sense that life isn't working as well as it used to, that something is wrong, that some energy has left our life. A man who always has survived in the world by charm and wit finds he's not as sharp as he used to be. A woman who has floated through the world with her goddess-like beauty cannot deny the wrinkles she sees in the mirror. The successful businessman no longer gets the same rush of energy by creating a new deal as he did in his younger days. Something is wrong. A sense of personal authorship is missing. And when there is no authentic authorship to living, the story begins breaking up, halting, lunging awkwardly toward a new chapter.

I know something of this loss of voice at a personal level. Part of my work as a minister is to deliver sermons each Sunday in the worship services of my church. I've learned through the years how to do this fairly well. I've learned what will work and what won't work in a sermon. Not too heavy. A little humor. Throw in a few timely quotes. I've become an expert at filling out twenty minutes each Sunday morning.

In 1995, I had this nagging feeling that something was not working. I was preparing my sermons. I was preaching each week. People came out and said the perfunctory "nice sermon" to me, but under the heaviness of my robe and stole I knew something was wrong.

At the time, I was participating in a monthly ecumenical preaching seminar. This group consisted of other ministers, two of whom preached each month in front of the seminar. Afterward we would offer suggestions and a critique of the sermons. In November 1995, I preached for the seminar. During my presentation I had this strange experience of actually hearing myself. I was delivering this sermon, and suddenly I could feel my deepest and truest self step aside from my body. What I saw was this person blathering on and on and on. That person was me. I heard his voice. I saw his body. And I knew that it was both me and not me. I could hear me talking, but my true self just looked at him and said, "Who in the world is this? What are you saying? That's not really you, is it?"

At the very moment this happened, I looked out to my colleagues sitting in the old, cavernous sanctuary, and two of them, at exactly the same moment, crossed their arms and legs. Their unconscious signs were obvious. They were closing off. Shutting down. It's as if they had put up some invisible shield to protect themselves from the sermon, the message, and, the truth be told, probably from me.

I don't know how to say it in any other way except that I felt the death of my own voice at that moment. I finished the sermon, grinding all the way to the end. I sat through the critique. But I might as well have been sitting in a tent by myself at the North Pole. I was dead, and I was gone, and, yes, I too was screaming.

After months of reflection, what I've concluded is that this boyish need to please and have everyone admire and like me, especially at the moments when I deliver sermons, was dying. What died was the need to strain, to rise up in a pitch high within my throat, and to say the things that I'm expected to say—which may or may not have anything to do with my deepest sense of authenticity. A new voice was trying to come to life within me. I wrote the next day in my journal: "I will not say that which I do not believe. I will only speak out of my deepest authenticity. I will learn to have fun and delight in what I'm saying and with those to whom I say it. I will try to move aside and let a deeper voice of Spirit come out of my body." It didn't dawn on me until later that this death and birth of a voice happened on November 28. My birthday. Interesting? Hmm.

A few weeks later I had a dream about my dog, Lucy. Lucy is a beautiful black Labrador whom I'll tell you more about later in the book. But in this dream I was looking down and talking to Lucy, and Lucy was talking to me. I thought, *That's neat! A talking dog.* I asked her, "How are you?" And she said, "I'm fine. How are you?" Dreams can be very strange.

I turned around for a moment, and someone cut off Lucy's head. It wasn't gory or bleeding. Just a perfectly severed head. I reached down and picked up her head up, and it continued talking to me. "Wow," she said, "this is weird, isn't it?"

I said, "I've got to get your head back on your body."

I then tried my best to connect the talking head with the body. I tried repeatedly to do this. But over and over again the head rolled off to the floor. I looked at her and said, "I don't know what I'm going to do. I don't know how to put you together." And then I awoke.

That dream, like my experience of preaching for my seminar group, has become a haunting narrative for me. Dreams, viewed from a certain perspective, are like another form of stories. I have since reflected that it's not easy to connect the mind and the heart, the voice and the body. It's not easy to create a story that is whole, authentic, real. Just as a voice died, so another was trying to come to life. What has become severed in me? Cut off? What spiritual connection do I need to make to be deeply alive? These are the questions I listen to as I try to compose the story of my life.

 Spiritual aliveness begins by listening to our story. To say we are too busy is not good enough. To say that we're not used to this kind of life-reflective living is also unacceptable. I'm not suggesting some kind of spiritual or psychological self-absorption. We need the stories of others too. But we need to begin and end with listening to our own story. In this listening process, we may conclude that it's time to bring certain chapters to a close. But, more important, we will feel the possibility of calling new chapters into being. At the heart of life is an ecstatic newness waiting to be born within us.

Yes, You Are Invited

Part of the power of stories is their invitational quality. To me that is the difference between stories and maxims. I hear maxims all the time:

QUIT SMOKING
LOSE WEIGHT
GO TO CHURCH
BE A NICE PERSON
JUST DO IT

Maxims become billboards and bumper stickers. But they also become walls. When you read a billboard, all you do is stand in front of it, have the message slap you in the face in take-it-or-leave-it fashion, and then walk away.

Stories, however, become doors. They say: "Welcome." "Enter here." "We've been expecting you." In this sense, stories grant us permission to try on new possibilities and explore new worlds. When I heard Dan Wakefield begin unraveling the tale of his own spiritual story, it was not at all like standing in front of a wall reading a maxim. He was opening a door, inviting me in, asking me to listen to him and, just as important, to listen to myself. And in the same way, you too may know the feeling of losing your voice. Maybe that story awakens in you a slumbering spiritual awareness. Or maybe you have a David Bobo or a David Steindl-Rast in your life, and hearing stories about them awakens some forgotten joy of relationship. Stories invite, lure, persuade. No force. No coercion. They engage participation by opening the doors of the imagination.

This invitational quality of stories came home to me recently when I read in Hillary Rodham Clinton's book *It Takes a Village* the story of how she, then-Governor Clinton, and their daughter, Chelsea, had the funny experience of trying to break open a coconut in the driveway of the governor's mansion in Little Rock. They tried everything to break this elusive coconut, but it kept rolling and bouncing away. For the Clinton family, this has become one of those funny, ordinary stories that they tell and retell. It helps them laugh at themselves. It gives them a comical sense of family ethos. And, most of all, the sheer act of recalling and smiling lightens the stress of their now supercharged, stressful lives.

When I read that story, I remembered a childhood experience visiting my Aunt Jane in Cincinnati. For me, growing up in a small town in southern Indiana, a trip to Cincinnati might as well have been a trip to another planet. This was the big city. Filled with big city sounds—fire engines, police cars, roaring traffic. Home of the Cincinnati Reds! I remember the smells. I remember thinking the houses were so close together. I remember seeing so many people, many of them of a different color. To a ten-year-old boy, this was an utterly new and fascinating world.

And they also had supermarkets. I had never seen a supermarket. My grandma and grandpa owned a small grocery store, A&G Market, and that's where we got our groceries. But Cincinnati had supermarkets. The first time I went into the Kroger store near my aunt's house, I couldn't believe it. They had everything. Everything! So many groceries. So many aisles. They even had people talking on a PA system— "Price check in produce, please." This was surely the brave, new world.

And that's where I saw my very first real, genuine, fresh coconut. It was big and brown and hard. I picked it up and felt the stringy, bark-like texture in my hands. I shook it and could hear the milk inside. I had heard of coconut milk and, of course, I had seen coconuts in movies and television shows. Yes, I watched *Gilligan's Island*. But actually to go to the store and buy a coconut was just too much. It felt, well, it felt exotic.

I asked my aunt if I could buy the coconut, and she said yes. I took it back to her house, and I remember drilling a hole in the end and draining all the coconut milk into a glass. I drank it that afternoon. I then took a hammer and cracked open the coconut in her basement. She helped me take a knife and carve out pieces of coconut. I must have chewed and chewed and chewed all day on coconut. I also learned why people buy coconut already shredded and in plastic bags. Much easier.

That coconut became for me a symbol of a bigger world. I could feel the world get bigger with every taste of that coconut. There was more to life than Grandma and Grandpa's little grocery store. More to the world than Salem, Indiana, population five thousand, with one working stoplight. With that coconut the world felt limitless and extraordinary, and what I had not even imagined became possible.

Hillary Rodham Clinton has no idea that her story of the coconut invited such memory for me. But it did. And that's the power of story. Stories themselves become the coconuts that make the world big, beautiful, and daring. Ah, the wonderful difference between reading a sign plastered on a billboard and hearing someone say, "Once a upon a time…" Sometimes it's the difference, not between life and death, but between deadness and aliveness.

The Stories That Hold Us Together

I'm not sure if my Aunt Jane remembers the coconut the way I do, but what I know is that stories hold families together. Part of the crisis in our families today is that we don't have time to create the stories and then retell them again and again. We go off to separate televisions strategically placed throughout the house, watch different channels, and then wonder why we never talk or why we seemingly have nothing to talk about. We plug in with the portable CD player, go on walks with the Walkman hanging from our ears, or hold on to the joystick of Super Nintendo and are puzzled why relationships in our families aren't as satisfying as we would like.

I agree with those who say there is a moral crisis in our family life. But the crisis does not merely involve teaching the traditional elements of morality. This is where the self-appointed czar of American moral life, William Bennett, doesn't go far enough. Teaching morality only scratches the surface of the problem. Besides, morality without satisfying relationships leads only to a deadly and oppressive legalism. The crisis we face is relational. We don't talk to each other. We don't listen to each other. We don't spend time with each other. And the missing piece of the puzzle for more and more families today is the sharing of common stories.

The stories families need to share cut in two distinct directions. First are stories of joy and meaning that beg to be shared again and again in families. I was driving down the road a few months ago, and a song by Eric Clapton titled "Tears in Heaven" came on the radio. Immediately, all three of my kids said simultaneously, "There's Dennis!" And behind that exclamation is a story.

I don't even remember Dennis' last name. All I remember was that it was Youth Sunday at my church. Youth Sunday is a senior minister's nightmare. You never know what the kids will do. That year the youth wanted to do it all—songs, prayers, music, sermon, communion. I came to church, took my place in a pew, and waited for the show to begin.

Dennis was thirteen years old and had a squeaky voice that couldn't make up its mind if it was going north or south. But Dennis had volunteered to do a solo at the church.

He took his place in front of the congregation, had a friend play the guitar, and started squeaking out the song "Tears in Heaven." I can still see him sitting on the stool, the music stand in front of him, and he sang:

Would you know my name,
    If I saw you in heaven.

Would it be the same,
    If I saw you in heaven.

And as he sang I could see the congregation begin to fidget. I started to fidget. I could feel myself turn red. I was embarrassed. Embarrassed for

Dennis. For the whole church. Not only was this song sounding awful, but at the pace Dennis was going, it would be two in the afternoon before he finished the song.

But Dennis kept right on singing:

I must be strong,
> And carry on.

Because I know I don't belong,
> Here in heaven.[4]

And just when I thought he would be unable to finish the song, somehow he found the courage and the breath and the last note to bring it to completion.

And when he finished, there was silence.

The kids in the youth group wanted to giggle; I could tell by looking at their faces. But even they were silent. And for a few seconds, it was one of those rare moments when the church just didn't know what to do. From a performance perspective, it was so meager.

But then something strange happened. It was as if we all had this simultaneous recognition of what *guts*—and that's the only word for it— it took for Dennis to do what he had done. Yes, we suffered through it. But so did he. And this mousey little kid sang this song because in his own way he loved God and had tried to bring a little of that love to others. He didn't care if he sounded a little foolish. All of us there that morning knew we had been in the presence of something deeply true and authentic.

It seemed that the silence lasted forever. And then someone, it had to have been his mother, started to applaud. And then everyone applauded. And then, to my utter amazement, they all stood and applauded. To top it all off, Dennis got off his stool, and right before the entire congregation, he took the biggest bow I've ever witnessed. Amazing!

Now, it's just a story. One little slice of life experience I happened to witness with my wife and three children. But, in a strange way, that's one of the stories that holds our family together. We hear that song on the radio and say, "There's Dennis." (Sorry, Eric Clapton.) And by saying that, we are saying, "Remember that moment of transparent authenticity? Remember that moment when we witnessed courage? Remember that moment when we saw what church and faith are really all about? Remember that time when we wanted to laugh and cry at the same time? Do you remember? Let's not ever forget it!"

I sometimes listen in awe when I'm with families in their most delicate moments. Sickness. Death. Crisis. Invariably what happens is that families tell stories. Not maxims, but stories. Not even descriptions will do—"He was a good person." That's not enough. Instead, they tell stories of goodness or humor or sadness. It doesn't matter—they tell stories. "Do you remember the time . . .?" With those words, the glue that holds a family together is squeezed out, and families once again find a way of discovering meaning.

Some stories bring smiles to our face— "There's Dennis"—and become touchstones of aliveness and joy. Other stories, however, are harder to tell. These are the painful stories, the ones we want to keep secret. These are the stories that make us want to die. Yet, for the well-being of our families, we must tell them. Easy? Rarely. In the basement of most of our families live stories of secret shame or fear. Stories of guilt or failure. Stories of incidents and habits that beg not to see the light of public scrutiny. A mother's depression. A father's alcoholism. A child's shame of abuse. These are the stories most difficult to hear and tell.

In recent years, through the hard work of psychologists, therapists, and others in the healing professions, a cardinal rule has emerged: *The most difficult stories of our lives must be told.*

When Barbara came to see me in my office, I was surprised that she had even made the appointment. She was shy. Unassuming. She would show up at church from time to time but was one of those quiet people who went to great lengths not to make any ripples. In our first conversation she asked questions of trust.

"Will everything I say be in confidence?"

"Of course," I answered.

"And if I were to write you letters, do you open all your mail personally?"

Again, I offered an unhesitating "Yes."

She said, "I have some things to talk about that aren't easy for me to say."

I tried to assure her that I was unflappable about things and that if I felt uncomfortable about any conversation, I would let her know.

She hesitated, like a child ready to take her first jump off the high dive, and said, "I've done some things I'm not so proud of, you know. . . "

And with those words came the beginning of a long story, a life odyssey really, of one woman's experience of childhood sexual abuse, of promiscuity, of cycles of guilt and secret shame, of therapy and hospitalizations, and of more therapy. We talked once a week. Sometimes between visits she would write long letters filled with experiences and memories, feelings and emotions.

There were the tough theological questions such as: "Where was God?" "How could God allow this to happen?" "Can God really love me?" But what she needed from me was not a set of answers. She simply needed to tell her story. And looking back on that time, I also see that she needed me to pray for her each time we were together.

Yes, some of our family stories are difficult to hear and even more difficult to tell. But we must find the safe places and right places to tell our story. If we don't, we're destined to live in pain, perhaps even repeating the very behaviors that caused the pain in the first place. For many of us, our first response to the painful story is not to tell. Barbara's deepest fear was that telling would be more painful than not telling. Yet, slowly, mysteriously, telling the story heals the soul.

In this way, even the hard stories of our lives become touchstones. I'm still shaped today by hearing stories of the Great Depression from my grandfather. Stories of how he got up at four in the morning, sold donuts to factory workers, eking out any way he knew how a living for his family. I've heard the hard stories from Vietnam veterans—painful stories, stories easier not told than told. Yet, in the telling of the stories, we touch upon the healing we need to move forward into life. I listened to the hard stories of Barbara, but the telling of the story created for her the miracle of a new beginning. It's as if she was inviting herself to come back into her own life.

Whether painful or joyful, stories hold us together. But they must first be told, heard, and sometimes told again. In the telling of the stories of our lives, we find the spiritual energy to live.

Faith and Imagination

Unfortunately, many of us grew up with the idea that faith is a *set of beliefs* or a listing of *religious doctrines* in which we believe or with which we have intellectual agreement. For example, a Christian might say, "I believe in the virgin birth of Jesus" or "I believe in the doctrine of the Trinity." Those doctrines may or may not have anything to do with our experiential aliveness, and, sadly, aliveness is typically the last thing people associate with doctrines such as these. Because even if you affirm intellectually that such ideas are historically or religiously true, the so-what questions remain. *So what* if you believe in the virgin birth? *So what* if you believe in the Trinity? Or the five tenets of Calvinism? Or the Nicene Creed? Or the Apostles' Creed? The biggest religious question for all of us is "So what?" In the end, believing in something that doesn't bring life is not belief at all. That doesn't mean I have to understand everything in which I believe. That would be impossible. But belief is opening the door to personal and social transformation.

For some, the presence of these doctrines brings an essential structure to their human experience. At their best, such doctrines help define faith in a credible and life-giving way. Every major religion has its doctrines. Yet, for many others, these doctrines or beliefs are like trying to walk across the water while wearing concrete boots. The beliefs appeal only to our intellectual dimension, if they even appeal to that, and over and over again they become heavy-handed, authoritative, and almost always divorced from daily experience. Therefore, I can believe in the virgin birth of Jesus and still be as spiritually dead as a mall parking lot.

The theologian Paul Tillich correctly understood faith as something much more than agreement with a set of concepts, doctrines, or beliefs. In fact, Tillich would suggest that faith is a state of being ultimately concerned, or having a kind of passion for God.

I love that expression—*passion for God*—for it captures the essence of touchstones. Not just believing in God, but being engaged by God. Not just agreeing that there is a God, but participating in spiritual reality. Not having mere intellectual agreement with an abstract concept, but being engaged by and drawn to some infinite life and love that fills the universe. That's faith.

Frederick Buechner describes faith in this way: "Faith is the eye of the heart, and by faith we see deep down beneath the face of things—by faith we struggle against all odds to be able to see —that the world is God's creation even so. It is he who made us and not we ourselves, made us out of his peace to live in peace, out of his light to dwell in light, out of his love to be above all things loved and loving."[5]

Such *seeing* finally brings together faith and imagination in our experience. Not imagination as make-believe, but as a way of seeing, living, feeling. In this way, faith becomes the process of engagement with the dynamics of the universe. Not belief in a few creedal statements, but an existential dance with the deepest realities of life.

In her novel *Beloved*, Toni Morrison tells the story of Baby Suggs, who was the great matriarch of her family. The scene is a family gathering, a prime place for storytelling and the interplay of joy and sadness.

> After situating herself on a huge flat-sided rock, Baby Suggs, bowed her head and prayed silently. The company watched her from the trees. They knew she was ready when she put her stick down. Then she shouted, "Let the children come!" and they ran from the trees toward her.

"Let your mothers hear you laugh," she told them, and the woods rang. The adults looked on and could not help smiling.

Then "Let the grown men come," she shouted. They stepped out one by one from among the ringing trees.

"Let your wives and your children see you dance," she told them, and groundlife shuddered under their feet.

Finally she called the women to her. "Cry," she told them. "For the living and the dead. Just cry." And without covering their eyes the women let loose.

It started that way: laughing children, dancing men, crying women and then it got mixed up. Women stopped crying and danced; men sat down and cried; children danced, women laughed, children cried until, exhausted and riven, all and each lay about the clearing damp and gasping for breath. In the silence that followed, Baby Suggs, holy, offered up to them her great big heart.

She did not tell them to clean up their lives or to go and sin no more. She did not tell them they were the blessed of the earth, its inheriting meek or glorybound pure.

She told them that the only grace they could have was the grace they could imagine.[6]

In the stories of our lives, we find the grace we need to heal and help our lives. Indeed, telling and listening to these stories help us imagine an essential grace, a grace that finally lifts us above the mundane into a realm of meaning and well-being. They bring us to life. Just as a coconut can symbolize the infinite possibilities of the world to a small boy, or a teenager's squeaking out an Eric Clapton song can become a foolish moment of love and grace, so stories invite us into the rooms of our own lives and help us see ourselves, others, even the Divine in a new and remarkable way.

My son Matthew once asked me, "So, Dad, where *did* religion start?" Not a bad question coming from a then–third grader. There are a variety of answers to that question, some I like more than others, but surely one answer is that religion begins with a story. "So Abraham and Sarah left their land." And with that one opening, you have the beginning of a spiritual odyssey. "Buddha sat down underneath the gingko tree," and you have the beginning of religion. "Jesus went to the Jordan to be baptized by John," and religion begins again. Faith finally comes to us, not in maxims or beliefs, but in stories and tales and narratives.

So a Dan Wakefield "wakes up screaming," but screaming is not the total story. Narrative spins a web, connecting and crossing, stretching with just the right tension until it looks like a mystical mandela holding forth the promise of healing. Stories are about what happens. At least on the surface. But by diving down and hearing, really hearing, really telling the truth, stories become webs of meaning upon which we live our lives. We must listen, and we must tell, because if we can *imagine* it, we can come alive to it. And make no mistake, in the weaving of our life stories, we exercise a faith that far transcends what the traditional word "belief" might indicate. We come face to face with the possibility of new being and being new.

It's a Large World, After All

The world in which we live is a paradox. On the one hand, we experience the world as smaller than ever before in human history. Through radios, televisions, fax machines, and computers, the other side of the world is only a button away. I doubt if any of us fully recognize what a revolutionary effect this is having on the evolution of human consciousness. The explosion of information and factoids races through the human experience like a barrage of fireworks. We have the capacity to look through the window and understand virtually every living culture that exists.

On the other hand, our world seemingly splinters off, fractures down, and is torn apart by forces that pit one person against another or one group against another. Why is it that at precisely the moment the world is shrinking, its people are finding it ever more difficult to live together? Why, rather than relationships being enhanced by new technologies, do we feel the world is more tense, more menacing, and less conducive to the flowering of the human spirit? This is the paradox of our situation.

Perhaps the realization that needs to happen is that technology will *not* become the savior of the human family. As much as we would like to believe that there is a scientific answer for all our questions and a technological innovation for all our problems, a truth must be faced—namely, that as human beings we need something more than technology and science. This is not to disparage either. It is simply a matter of recognizing that the human spirit needs some healing, some touch, some experience that goes beyond the latest advancement of the day. Information is not the same as transformation.

It is at this point that I think the power of story asserts itself in a new way. Yes, there has been a technological revolution. But there also has been a narrative revolution, at the heart of which is the authentication of diverse story and experience. The unquestioned status of Western tradition has indeed been questioned. The white-male-Euro-American tradition has a story to be told. But it's not the only story. And that's the revolution.

There are stories of women, of blacks, of Asians, of Hispanics, of gays, of lesbians, of children, of elderly, of poor, of Jews, of Christians, of Muslims, of Buddhists, of…of…of…, and these stories need to be heard. More than that, these stories have the power to bring the human family together, simultaneously raising consciousness and healing wounds of consciousness. If the human family can be conceived of as a broken circle, then stories can complete the circle, fill the gaps, bring it around to fullness.

One awareness I have of stories, therefore, is that I need them because they help me see that the world is bigger than my own experience. That one insight—the world is bigger than my own experience—is crucial to the well-being of the planet. I will say more about this later in the book, but for right now it's enough to say that stories enlarge the heart, and the bigger the heart, the bigger the world, and the bigger the world, the greater the aliveness.

What is the meaning of this disturbing parochialism that threatens our world? Militia movements. Anti-government compounds located in Montana and Idaho. Apocalyptic enclaves in Waco, Texas. How can we understand the intensity of tribal fighting in Bosnia? The unending feud between Palestinians and Jews? How can I understand the city where I once lived, Louisville, Kentucky, so deeply divided between west end and east end, between black and white, between rich and poor?

Often we assume that if the story is not directly our own, we don't need to pay attention to it. But this kind of ignorance makes the world dangerous. The story of the African American man is not my story, but I need to hear a Ralph Ellison or a Richard Wright or a Spike Lee. The story of a woman is not my story, but I cannot ignore the story of a Bobbie Lee Mason or a Marge Piercy or an Alice Walker. The story of depression is not my story, but I need to hear the story of a William Styron or an Art Buchwald. The story of a Holocaust survivor is not my story, but I need to hear the story of a movie such as *Schindler's List* or listen to a storyteller such as Elie Wiesel. The story of a child is not my story, but I need to hear the stories that come from a Robert Coles or an Alice Miller.

The power of stories is that they invite us to see the world as large and meaningful. True, others approach life quite differently than I do. Nevertheless, my life experience is intensified when I can appreciate the stories of others. It just will not do to ignore the stories of others. Neither will it help to hate the stories of others. Unfortunately, this is the posture some take toward the diversity of stories in our world. Not content simply to focus on their own experience to the exclusion of others, they want to muffle all stories that project a vision of life different from their canon of experience. Sadly, some can tell their story only over against the story of others.

From my experience I see this with religious fundamentalists. Fundamentalists make two cardinal errors. First, they identify their truth with all the truth. The second mistake is that they believe that to be faithful to their story, they must diminish the stories of everyone else who differs with them. It's one thing to claim that God's light can shine through only one window; it's another to believe you must nail up plywood on all the other windows of the world because God's light won't shine through them anyway! I suppose that, from a certain perspective, fundamentalists can be admired for their conviction and fervor. At the same time, if their focus on a solitary story of meaning excludes and diminishes others, their perspective should be called into question.

Even as I write this chapter, the Ku Klux Klan is planning a rally on the courthouse steps of a major American city. Historically, the Klan has not been content merely to focus on its narrow and ugly story of supremacy. Members must add to that a hostile bigotry toward blacks, Jews, and others. They attempt through intimidation and violence to silence stories. The world is more dangerous because of exclusivistic groups such as these, not to mention impoverished because of their ignoring the possibilities of listening to others.

Does this mean that we have to agree with every story ever told? No. Does it mean that every story is appropriate for all people? No. Children, for example, aren't ready to hear some stories. Does this mean that all discernment of stories should be suspended in order to facilitate meaningful listening? No. We must learn to listen and discern, and at times we must say that this story is unacceptable for the well-being of the human family. Does this mean that we have to ignore some of the foundational stories of Western civilization in order to make room for diverse voices? No. Just as two wrongs don't make a right, so also ignoring the stories of white, male Europeans won't help the diverse stories of others to be told and heard.

But the overall principles remain: The world is larger than we think. The more we can hear the diverse stories of our world, the more intense our life experience becomes. We need the stories of others to make the world a more livable planet. In the hearing and telling of stories comes the power of aliveness to heal and transform human life. The transformation we need can begin in many places and can be found in several different experiences, but one place where it almost always can be discovered is when our ears perk up, our eyes open wide, and another human being says to us, "Let me tell you a story. . . ."

Chapter 3

Rituals: Making Our Meaning

I remember Amherst, Massachusetts, the way Jacob remembered angels climbing up and down the ladder of his dreams; the soul longs for sacred ground.

I remember walking through the small New England village, stopping at Judy's delicatessen for a beer and corned beef sandwich, reading the newspaper while I sat alone at the table. I walked past the Jeffrey Amherst bookstore and smelled pipe smoke wafting from the front door. I looked up at the Congregational church, standing tall with its steeple pointing toward God and its black shutters looking like something Ted Williams used to wear under his eyes as he took graceful swings on a sunny day at Fenway Park. Across the street were tall evergreens hiding the home where Austin Dickinson, Emily's brother, lived and reared his family. A few more steps down the street and then I saw it, the reason why I'd traveled a thousand miles. It was the house of Emily Dickinson.

The red brick running from foundation to roof, the black door, the windows veiled with white lace sheers, all were cast in perfect colonial style. The roof was slate. Concrete steps started at the sidewalk and led all the way to the front door. The gardens were also there. In July they were in full bloom, with sunflowers stretching their necks toward light. Roses and zinnias were there too, with heavy, bulbous bees buzzing in systematic activity. The old benches invited a rest, a pause, but I didn't come here just to sit.

In fact, I wasn't sure why I was here.

When I graduated from seminary, my soul was parched. Grinding through books and papers had caused something inside me to dry up. We

53

all reach dry places in our lives. Sometimes we find ourselves living there for a long time. For reasons I still cannot fully explain, I turned to the poetry of Emily Dickinson. I needed images, words, but not just any words. I needed words that would gently carry me into life again, the way butterflies land effortlessly upon old woodpiles long forgotten behind barns. I wanted to feel something. Experience something. I was tired of analyzing life. I was tired of explaining life. I was tired of instructing other people about their lives. I wanted to taste life, smell life, swill it around in my mouth, then swallow it with ravenous joy. Henry David Thoreau once said, "I want to suck the very marrow out of life." Yes! I wanted the well-written line, not the meandering paragraph. I needed the artful ellipsis, not the footnoted explanation. I needed the insightful metaphor, not the airtight argument. It's not that I didn't appreciate academic life. I did. Still do. It's simply that I was hungry for something else.

Emily Dickinson wrote nearly two thousand poems. Incidentally, only seven of them were published in her lifetime. But in one year I read every one of them. Poem after poem. Image after image. Some, frankly, I didn't understand—like punch lines of a joke—I just didn't get it. But it didn't matter. I read on. Line after line. No titles. No sections. Just page after page of numbered poems, some of them no bigger than a piece of scratch paper. I've written longer grocery lists. But as I read them I felt a deep, soulful quality in my life begin to stir again. Slowly, deliberately, like a bear awakening in spring, I could feel myself coming back to life.

Yet there was more to it than simply reading the poems. I found myself in relationship with her presence. Invisible? Yes. Beyond touch? Of course. Nevertheless, I felt Emily as real in my life, sometimes more real and more present than the people who were living inside my house or working at my office. It was a kind of communion that I felt with her. A sacrament of grace and love that strangely sustained me in a dry time.

As I walked around the house, I thought of her fierce creativity and unnerving solitude. I wondered how she could hold the gold of her poetry so closely to her life. I felt myself walking on sacred ground. Why didn't her brilliance just blow the house apart the way tornados do in Kansas? Why didn't her bedroom, her small writing desk, her wooden chest where she hid her poetic scraps just spontaneously ignite into flames and burn the entire town down? I didn't know. But what I did know is that she had a spiritual intensity that I both wanted to touch and be touched by. Not just her knowledge of language, but her knowledge of living is what I wanted to feel.

I stood underneath the window of her bedroom. It was hot and humid, the way July is supposed to be in central Massachusetts. No breeze was blowing. I looked up at the window and imagined how many times she would part the curtains during the day just for a quick glimpse at the town. She didn't need much of the world. I suppose you don't when your inner world is so rich and full. She insightfully wrote in one of her poems, "I dwell in Possibility / A Fairer-House than prose. . ."

Standing on the front lawn, looking at her window, I saw something happen. Barely perceptible at first, but it happened as surely as my heart is beating while I write this sentence. The curtains in her bedroom window moved. Only slightly. But they moved. Was it some mysterious breath? Some mystical presence? I don't know, but I know they moved. It was only a brief moment. And then it was over.

Recalling that day in Amherst, I now realize that I was enacting a spiritual ritual. For centuries people have made their ritual pilgrimages to holy places, places infused with meaning and value. And in these places, people have wanted to walk upon some version of holy ground, to see holy sights, to be touched by holy angels, or to find some holy healing that would eventually move them forward into life. Ancient Jews would walk for miles on dusty roads, chanting psalms, praying prayers, telling stories of the faith, and making their way to Jerusalem because Jerusalem was a sacred space. But the pilgrimage to Jerusalem was just as sacred as arriving at Jerusalem. And so were the ritualistic preparations for getting on the road to get to Jerusalem. And don't forget, the going home after the last horn had been sounded and the final blessing uttered was a mean-ingful ritual too.

A Christian longs for the magic of a Christmas Eve mass in Rome. On the one hand, it makes no sense. The crowds. The babble of languages. You can barely see the pope, you know. But none of that matters to the ritual pilgrim. You want to go because you want to go, and wanting to go is enough. And not being able to explain why you want to go is all right too. Because this wanting, this hunger to go, is a spiritual impulse to find God or life or meaning or value, however those words fill themselves out in definition. Pilgrimage is ritual, and ritual is radically essential to the human experience.

Louis Charpentier provides an amazing description of those who have made the ritual journey to Chartres Cathedral. He writes: "Let us spare a thought for those who, century after century, took the pilgrim's staff, whether they were pagan or Christian, and set out by roads which were hardly tracks, across rivers that were hardly fordable, through forests where the wolf hunted in packs, through marshes of shifting mud in which poisonous water snakes lurked; subjected to rain, wind storms, sharp hail, sunstruck or frozen, at night the only shelter a flap of their

tunic pulled over the head; all this having left home and family not knowing if they would see them again, in order to reach at least once in their
lives a place where divinity dwelt."[1]

No, I didn't face any storms or poisonous snakes in Amherst, Massachusetts. And a stay at the nearby Red Lion Inn in Stockbridge repre-
sented no hardship compared with the ancient pilgrims who risked their
lives just to step foot into the great cathedral of Chartres. Yet there is a
continuity with their quest and my quest, as well as the quest of everyone
who ever has taken an intentional step to rediscover his or her spiritual
aliveness. We are pilgrims together, enacting a ritual of spiritual significance.

Rituals: A Working Definition

Like stories and relationships, rituals define what it means to be a
human being. They become touchstones to our aliveness, both individually and collectively. We participate in rituals—sometimes consciously, at
other times unconsciously—but we forever are participating in their hope
and magic.

One definition of ritual might be: *Any action we undertake to give our
lives spiritual depth and meaning.*

In his book *The Magic of Rituals*, Tom Driver makes the point that
there are "big" rituals and "small" rituals. Big rituals include actions such
as a family observance of Passover, sharing in the eucharist, a wedding
ceremony, a graduation, a funeral, or celebrating a Christmas holiday. These
are the big moments of life in which we participate. These ritual moments give our lives structure, and through them the wells of human
experience are dug deeper.

In our family, for example, Christmas is an important ritual holiday. It
transcends gift giving or gift getting. Christmas is a renewal time for our
family. Therefore, the simple act of picking out our Christmas tree has
become important to our entire family. Until we moved recently, we had
gone to the same Christmas tree farm for the past ten years. We go out to
a field and pick it out. After much debate and conversation and evaluation, we pick it out. And then that night we have a little party—my wife
and I and our three children—and decorate the tree. Usually there's a fun
debate over who has the right to take credit for finding the beautiful tree.
And while we decorate the tree, we play Christmas music, eat some of
our favorite snacks, and simply enjoy, if only for a few hours, the essential
meaning of being a family. It's not a spectacular kind of evening, but it is
meaningful.

For me at least, this ritual must go back to my own childhood because I have fond memories of bringing the Christmas tree home with

my dad. In fact, one rude awakening I'll never forget was when I came home for my first Christmas after having been away at college. I walked into the living room and was shocked to see that my family already had gotten the Christmas tree without me. How dare they! How dare they leave me out of this important experience! They left me out of this defining ritual, and, strangely, I knew at that moment that I was no longer a member of my family in the same way I had been for my first eighteen years of living. Not participating in the ritual signaled an important transition from childhood to adulthood and, to some extent, from insider to outsider.

I see my own family, now, feeling this mysterious connection to rituals. Year after year we have our family Christmas dinner on Christmas Eve night. And, of course, after our holiday meal there's church. I cannot imagine Christmas Eve without this ritual of worship. It all speaks to me. The lighting of the Christ candle. The music. Sharing the eucharist together. Hearing words such as "This is my body; this is my blood"—these words speak to me in deep and powerful ways. The words themselves are ritualistic, having been uttered for more than two thousand years. Yet, on Christmas Eve, they feel new. Just hearing the Christmas story read from Luke's Gospel defines me, inspires me, breathes new life into me. Certain phrases in that reading become a kind of soulful music. "Wrapped him in swaddling clothes…This will be a sign to you…Glory to God in the highest…" These words, having their own drama, become part of an even bigger ritualistic drama of the holiday.

Christmas is a big ritual. Passover is a big ritual. National holidays are big rituals. Undertaking a pilgrimage is a big ritual. My concern, however, is that for many of us in our culture, even the big rituals are being reduced and marginalized in the lives of people, and thus the opportunity for our spiritual aliveness also is reduced. Big ritual is not the same as big shopping, big spending, and big consumption. Big ritual is not the same as a three-day weekend from work, to which, unfortunately, many of our national holidays have been reduced. All you have to do is walk through the malls of any city, and what you witness are numb, exhausted, joyless people walking from store to store, expressionless, as bland as the merchandise they are buying. Big ritual is not the same as a big production, a big extravaganza, a big show.

Most of us, I'm afraid, need to become ritual archeologists and begin recovering and restoring the importance of big rituals in our communities and families. If we don't, not only do our own lives begin drying up, but the lives of our children and grandchildren become aimless and empty as well. Big rituals are essential to our human aliveness.

Yet, as important as big rituals are, small rituals also play a part in our daily spiritual vitality. Small rituals tend to be more idiosyncratic to persons or families. Nevertheless, they provide meaningful structures for our existence. A small ritual might be as simple as reading to a child before she goes to bed each night. Think of the utter loveliness of giving a child beautiful words before she slips into a night of slumber. Kissing your spouse good-bye in the morning as you leave for work is a small ritual. Grinding coffee beans, drinking coffee, and reading the newspaper in the morning is a little ritual that brings pleasure and delight. Calling a long-distance friend once a month is a nice ritual. My wife's mother calls our house every Saturday at 8:00 a.m.; it's a small ritual that holds our family together. As soon as the phone rings, I always say, "I'm sure that's your mother." And it is. Some people write in a journal each day. That's a ritual.

Ernest Boyer, Jr., describes a wonderful ritual—or what he sometimes calls "a little gesture"—that he and his wife created when they were first married. When they were students in Japan, they found a piece of pottery, a small cup really, that they both came to love. It's always amazing to me what the soul is drawn to—a piece of pottery, an antique lamp, a photograph found in some obscure gallery on vacation. They wanted to buy the cup, but the potter said it wasn't for sale, that he was sorry, but it was a mistake that it had been placed in the window. He explained that they no longer made that particular cup and that he just couldn't bring himself to sell it.

Yet the potter did something even more extraordinary. He opened the case, picked up the cup, and said, "Please accept it as a gift." It was too precious to sell, but it was perfect to give as a gift. Isn't that absolutely wonderful? It's true, I think, that the best rituals in our lives rarely cost anything in terms of dollars and cents. At their heart, rituals are free.

Throughout their marriage, the Boyers have used this treasured piece of pottery as their "waiting cup." When one of them has to be out of town and away from the family, the other one uses the cup. It becomes a gentle reminder that the other person is gone, and a symbol of waiting for his or her return. Often the cup isn't used for long stretches of time, but when leaving is necessary, the cup is taken off the shelf and used. In this ritual, both a story and a relationship become a living presence for this couple.

Now, that may not seem like a big ritual, this ritual of the waiting cup. And, in one sense, it's not. It doesn't compare to the depth of meaning found in a big ritual, such as the celebration of the eucharist, nor is it as far-reaching as a national day of mourning, such as we had after the bombing of the federal building in Oklahoma City. Yet these little rituals, human gestures of intentional actions designed to help us find meaning, can become important touchstones for our living.

Regarding rituals as touchstones, it's important that our thinking open up to the power of rituals in our lives. Think about it for a moment and ask yourself: What big rituals are available to me that I've been missing? When's the last time I really celebrated Memorial Day or Veterans Day? When's the last time I made my way to the cathedral to partake in the mass? When's the last time our family planned a reunion? When's the last time we really celebrated a person in our family? When's the last time I attended a class reunion? When's the last time I experienced the high holidays at the synagogue?

At some point in our lives, the big rituals of human existence need to make a claim upon us, become important to us, because when they do, an amazing flow of spiritual meaning and satisfaction becomes available to us. We need to join our lives to them. Make ourselves available to them. Be touched by them.

Key to the ritual process is attentiveness. Most of us are busy, living demanding lives, finding ourselves moving at a pace previous generations would have found unimaginable. Yet, the very essence of our humanity and the humanity of the communities where we live hinges upon our participation in ritual. The quality of attentiveness we bring to our lives, both individually and collectively, many times determines the spiritual satisfaction we discover in our living.

And in terms of small rituals we need to ask, What little gestures do I already do to give my life meaning? Perhaps we don't have to invent anything. We already may be all-star ritual makers. But the little gestures are crucial to our spiritual growth, and in no way are the possibilities for new rituals ever exhausted. What new rituals could I create to enhance my life? What new rituals could I create for my most important relationships? What new rituals might bring me closer to the people of the world? I know one family who, when they go to the grocery store, buy one sack of groceries for the local food bank. They do this every week. What a wonderful ritual. Imagine what that teaches the children in that family, let alone the contribution it makes to the hungry. The small rituals of our living become touchstones for our well-being and the well-being of others. Whether big or small, the need to ritualize is one of the most spiritual, deeply human endeavors of our existence.

In their book *Leading with Soul,* Lee Bolman and Terrence Deal suggest, "When ritual and ceremony are authentic and attuned, they fire the imagination, evoke insight, and touch the heart. Ceremony weaves past, present, and future into life's ongoing tapestry. Ritual helps us face and comprehend life's everyday shocks, triumphs, and mysteries."[2] I believe their evaluation of ritual is exactly right. For to have the imagination fired, as they suggest, or the heart touched, is to be radically alive.

We Are All Religious

At the heart of human experience is the experience of being religious. It is not that some people are religious and others are not. To be human is to be religious. Religious experience is about ultimacy, and it is true, I think, that every person longs for this sense of the ultimate. Maybe it is a longing for home in the vastness and randomness of the universe. Or perhaps we want to know ourselves as part of a larger narrative, to feel ourselves as significant characters in the unfolding plot of the world. Or maybe we want to stand upon some sacred ground, feel the dirt between our toes, know ourselves as fully human beings, radically alive, radically whole, radically at one with the universe. In our quest as human beings, we want significance, love, and a feeling of personal authorship for our living.

I know that going to Amherst was not an explicitly religious pilgrimage—at least it wouldn't appear so on the surface. At the same time, I would suggest that it was just as *religious* as any pilgrimage to Jerusalem or Mecca. I enacted a ritual journey in search of ultimacy. What I wanted at that point in my life is still beyond any rational articulation, but it was for me a journey that proceeded from the deepest place in my heart. Viewed in this way, it's clear to me that our entire culture is in some way religious. Some persons search for ultimacy through explicitly religious actions such as going to church, practicing meditation, or turning toward Mecca and praying each day. These actions we quickly acknowledge as religious.

Yet there is also "religious" expression found in the malls that now clutter the American landscape. The progression of America is curious. We once built cathedrals. Then factories. Then skyscrapers. Now we build the Mall of America, and people plan their vacations around shopping, consuming, and glittering entertainment. Nothing is wrong with shopping per se, but the obsessive consumerism of our nation indicates that there is a longing inside the American soul more far-reaching than the mere purchase of an item from a store. Look at the role entertainment is now playing in our culture. Neil Postman argues that the psychological capital of the United States has become Las Vegas. Glitz. Play. Entertainment. And it goes on and on and on, continuously, nonstop, twenty-four hours a day. Sports, once a pastime, has become part of the entertainment industry. Not long ago, sporting teams were able to produce heroes such as Joe DiMaggio or Mickey Mantle. Now media creations such as "Shaq" or "Air" Jordan are individual corporations marketed to the insatiable appetite of public consumption.

The question many of us face—and if we're not facing it, we should be—is the question of the adequacy of our life meaning. After all, we can be season-ticket holders and watch the Chicago Bulls from the best seats in the house and still be utterly empty. We can shop 'til we drop and still be dead on the inside. Yet, in all our endeavors, even the misdirected ones, there is an underlying desire to find ultimacy. This is the religious quest. There is some chalice inside every human being wanting to be filled with new wine. Therefore, it's not the case that we have to think about becoming religious as much as it is that we have to awaken to our religious nature and then direct our religious longings in the most meaningful way possible.

And if we are religious, then it is also true that we are ritualizers. When I see basketball fans at the University of Kentucky painting their faces blue and white, waving flags, and doing musical chants, I'm convinced that ritual is part of the human experience. It is a sight to behold! Or when I speak at a Rotary luncheon and watch the old men rise to pledge their allegiance to the flag, I see them for what they are—ritualizers, every single one of them. A bride who can barely afford a wedding in the first place works two jobs and borrows money just so she can wear that long, flowing wedding dress of her dreams. It's all about ritual.

I am, therefore I ritualize.

Robert Fulghum offers the following insights about ritual:

Every human being asks the elemental religious questions: Who am I? What am I doing here?…What is the meaning of my life? How do I account for the awesome, mysterious majesty of the universe, and what is my place in the scheme of things?…The ritual moments of life mark changes from moment to moment, day to day, year to year, and from one stage of being to another. The conscious acknowledgments of these changes are called rites of passage. Sometimes we celebrate in public, sometimes in private, and most often, in secret. Sometimes we are aware of the importance of the moment and at other times its importance is established later, through the ritual of remembering.[3]

This union of ritual and religion opens new doors for many of us. The hallmark characteristic of the Baby Boomer generation has been intense spiritual longing coupled with an equally intense disdain of organized religion. Almost all the polls tell the same story. Do you believe in God? "Yes!" Do you go to church or synagogue? "No!" There exists a free-floating spirituality in our culture, amorphous and ghostlike, that is as hard to pin down as nailing a piece of gelatin to the wall. As an article in the *New York Times* recently concluded, "God has been de-centralized." Yet, as beautiful as it is to float in a hot air balloon, freely moved by the wisps of spiritual wind, there comes a time when the balloon must take off, find direction, and eventually land.

Could it be that this very intersection of meaning and ritual—the take-offs and landings of spiritual process—offers an invitation to our culture to take a new look at organized religion? A new look at the mass, for example? A renewed participation in the Sabbath? A longing to be a recipient of baptism? The possibility of weekly religious practice? Formal religious life, rather than being a stone fortress of hierarchies and traditions, might be the very place where the richest rituals are available to human experience. And maybe it's the case that some of the drifting, blue-funk listlessness that has captured many of our teenagers might be addressed by a community grounded in ultimacy and ritual. The fact that human beings practice ritual, even at an unconscious level, is an indication that the human soul longs for religious community.

The Sacred Wedding

Rituals are spiritual touchstones because they become moments when the interior and exterior realities of life are brought together in sacred marriage. Most days we find ourselves living split, divided lives, and the result of this split is anxiety and meaninglessness. The fact that we feel this anxiety is a sign that we want wholeness, but finding it often proves to be elusive.

In some ways it is misleading to talk about exterior and interior realities because all reality is finally seamless and one. But these designations can be helpful as we move toward a more soulful life.

I recently performed the ritual of a wedding for a couple. I do this frequently for couples. This was a second marriage for both Ron and Joan. They are in their mid-forties, and both have lived long enough to be acquainted with the grief side of life. Yet on the day of their wedding, they were beaming with joy. Unlike so many younger couples who are interested in the glamorous production of the wedding ceremony—often looking like Barbie and Ken for the video camera—or in trying to recreate a fantasy out of the most recent bridal magazine, Ron and Joan were in touch with the simple joy of bringing their lives together in this ceremony of marriage.

Union. The very word is powerful, isn't it? To be in union, to feel union, to experience union. Belonging is at the heart of the human experience. In the ritual of Ron and Joan's wedding, I had a strong feeling that a sacred union of inner and outer worlds was taking place. In the outer world, they were speaking vows, exchanging rings, and lighting a unity candle. He wore a nice suit. For her part, she walked down the aisle carrying a lovely bouquet of flowers. But in that outward ritual of union was the joining together of their inner lives. Inner feminine and inner masculine were brought into union. The mythic qualities of bride and groom were being intertwined. The distinct energies of their respective souls were brought together, as well. None of this, of course, was seen with the physical eye, but a real spiritual union was taking place nevertheless. Lovers sometimes speak of finding their "soul mate." Such an expression comes from the territory of the sacred marriage.

In ancient cultures, the ritual of initiation was significant because of this very union between inner and outer realities. When a child was "ritualized" through circumcision, for example, that child became intimately related to the entire history of Judaism. Putting aside the contemporary medical and psychological questions such a practice now raises, the meaning of the ritual remains undeniable. Circumcision wasn't just a personal moment. Nor was it merely a family moment. This ritual became a connecting moment to all the hopes and heartbreak of Jewish experience. It was big ritual and little ritual rolled into one. The child became spiritually connected with all the heroes of faith such as Abraham and Sarah. The child became part of the plot line in the stories of slavery and exodus. Such an initiatory ritual created a sacred marriage between a child and the complete ethos of a people.

One way to imagine the function of ritual is this: You're standing on the banks of the Mississippi River. On one side, you feel the external reality of daily living. Bills that need to be paid. Children that must be clothed, fed, and educated. A job that demands more and more of your time and creativity. This is daily life, and this is the side of the river on which most of us live. We find that we often are moved along by the events of the world and, on occasion, actually initiate events of our own choosing.

Yet, as you look across this mighty river, its waters whisper, flow and whisper, sing some lilting whispering song about the possibility for your life. It is numinous and mysterious. Extraordinary and quiet. Some part of you is on the other side, some piece of your psychological puzzle that you sense, even at times see, beyond the flowing waters. It's as if you see yourself, but it's not merely you, not the daily you, but the extraordinary possibility of what you might become. And like the sirens of old that would beckon travel and voyage and pilgrimage, you too sense a call and long to be united with that which is most essential to your depth as a person.

Victor Turner talks about the importance of liminality when it comes to understanding ritual. By liminality he means that space in between, that place in life where we know what we've been, but it's unclear what we are going to become. Crossing over the Mississippi River is liminal territory. And, therefore, the point of ritual is to help us transition to new parts of our being.

Which, of course, is what God is about in the world. The very word *religion* means to bind back or to bind together. A religious experience is one of those moments when we feel united to that which is ultimate and meaningful in life. Understandably, ritual has been crucial to religion because religion revolves around a depth connection with the divine. And, I would suggest, every ritual—even the most ordinary ones, such as the first cup of daily coffee or the kiss good-bye or the nightly prayer—can be understood as religious expression.

These rituals should never be underestimated. For many of us today and for the well-being of our children, we need to recover certain rituals. In other cases, there awaits the opportunity to create rituals. Yet the importance of them can hardly be overstated. One issue that many of our children and young adults are facing today is a lack of ritual experience and, consequently, the isolating experience of never adequately connecting their inner and outer realities. They long for a sacred marriage but rarely are able to speak of it in this way. There is a mystical, magical quality to ritual, and unless we find ways to touch the touchstone quality of them, we are destined for little more than existential loneliness.

Ritual and Institutional Life

I want to suggest that, in addition to the importance of rituals in personal life, rituals also are essential in the various institutions of our lives. Institutional life defines the soul's journey too. Maybe we're an accountant in a large corporation or perhaps a nurse working in a major hospital. We might own an insurance agency but find ourselves working in a network of relationships with the folks at the home office, every move filled with political nuance and meaning. Many of us attended universities and colleges, and there we belonged to service clubs, sororities and fraternities, or professional organizations related to our field of study. We attend churches, work on a Junior League committee, help in the annual picnic for the neighborhood association, and the list goes on and on. Despite the myth of the lone American hero, we are people who live and work within the complexities of institutions and organizations.

Not surprisingly, institutions have their rituals too. In their book *Corporate Cultures: The Rites and Rituals of Corporate Life*, Terrence Deal and Allen Kennedy accurately make the point that "many rituals or ceremonies seem like a lot of hoopla. Yet the underlying purpose is very serious…"[4]

They describe one major American company's ritual of awarding an "Attaboy" award to the employee who has rendered extraordinary service in a project. This old Navy, back-patting ritual of "Attaboy" has become part of their corporate culture, and the ritual award continues to feed a cultural ethos in a positive way.

In Indianapolis, Indiana, an elementary school has held an annual science fair for more than twenty-five years. Each year, the teachers go into crisis mode trying to make sure everything goes well for the science fair. Parents and students panic over the pressure of meeting deadlines, not to mention the stress of competing for the honor of first place. The newspaper sends a reporter. A local celebrity, usually a weatherman, presides as master of ceremonies for the evening of judging and awarding. One particular year, someone—no doubt a new teacher—suggested they skip the science fair and adjust to an every-other-year schedule. The entire faculty was in an uproar. Even though it costs time and money and energy (the truth is the teachers complain bitterly about having to do the darn thing every year), the thought of canceling it was abhorrent to the entire faculty. And why? It had become a corporate ritual.

I would offer the following awarenesses regarding ritual and institutional life:

People need to be aware of what the essential rituals are in any organization. This is especially true of beginning new relationships with an organization. I know I have often underestimated the importance of institutional ritual. This is a mistake. Every institution is thick with story and language and ritual. Every organization—whether it be a family, church, synagogue, or a Fortune 500 corporation—has composed a dynamic array of rituals. To be effective in any organization, a person needs to understand this rich composition. Alas, the rituals found in organizations become touchstones for the central life and meaning of the organizations.

At the same time, I want to suggest that understanding the culture is not the same thing as endorsing it. There are corporate cultures, religious and educational institutions, clubs, and groups that frankly need to find new life. Sometimes culture must be challenged, recreated, and reconstituted in a way that makes sense. And the very power of creating corporate change often is related to the ability to create new rituals for the participants. One challenge of leadership is the appreciation for past rituals and the creativity to find new ones.

People need to be aware that rituals in any organization both work and don't work. All rituals have a down side. The eucharist can be mindless. A science fair can be oppressive. Yet, in most cases, rituals have an efficacious component to them too. As is the case with the human personality, there is both light and shadow, positive and negative. Appreciating the complex nature of ritual is essential. No one ritual finally functions perfectly as a touchstone, but just because it doesn't function perfectly doesn't mean that it doesn't function at all.

This insight is especially important for people who have come out of a highly ritualistic background. Many times their primary experience has been with the oppressive qualities of ritual. I have many friends who were brought up in the Roman Catholic Church, attended Catholic schools, and were part of a heavy Catholic culture. Now, there are many positive ways of framing their experience. But some—not all, but some—found the ritualized culture difficult, if not deadening, to their spiritual lives. For them, ritual has come to mean boring, passionless, laborious. This, of course, is not the intention of the Roman Catholic Church. I'm only pointing out what some have experienced. To those for whom the word ritual has come to be a pejorative word, I would suggest that there is a balance between understanding what ritual can and cannot do for the spiritual life. The negative experience of any ritual should not be allowed to mute the positive potential that other rituals might possesses.

People need to be aware that new rituals can be created. Tradition and rites are important, but even the best tradition was meant to be clay, not concrete. Each generation takes the clay, shapes it, and forms it until the magic of ritual comes to life again. Most organizations resist such creativity. Yet, at the same time, many people long for it, hope for it, even await someone with courage and creativity to step up and offer it. Creating new rituals is like the work of translation. Although a translation of an ancient text might have been excellent at the turn of the twentieth century, that doesn't necessarily mean that the translation will serve the twenty-first century adequately. Rituals are open for revision. Managing the polarities of stability and creativity is the art of leadership, if not the art of being human. In most cases, the risk of creativity is worth it.

It's hard to overstate the importance of ritual for organizations. Again in their book *Corporate Cultures*, Deal and Kennedy suggest that rituals are not only important, but also necessary. They tell the remarkable story of one company that hired a new manager. This manager was required to negotiate with the labor union every two years in a collective bargaining process. The young manager, eager to please, did his homework, went to the first meeting, and presented a contract to the workers that was far and away better than anything the labor leaders had hoped to receive. When he finished his presentation, he sat with a glow of satisfaction surrounding him. But only for a brief moment. The union leaders started lambasting the young manager for taking away their power, for undercutting the process, for trying to pull one over on the workers. They even accused him of trying to destroy the very value of negotiation that they had cherished through the years.

Their vigorous protest absolutely stunned the young manager. What had gone wrong? Why the uproar? Why was he so misunderstood? These were the questions racing through his mind.

What he had failed to understand was simple—it was a rite of passage in that corporate culture to fight, argue, negotiate, and then finally agree upon compensation. Agreeing was not nearly as important as getting to the agreement. The process itself had become a ritual. Unknowingly, he had undercut the importance of this ritual by shortcutting the process, even if it was with a remarkable degree of efficiency. It is true that rituals are not only important to the spiritual transformation of organizations; they are essential.

Back to the Pilgrimage

I started this chapter with the ritual of pilgrimage, and now I come back around to it. All of life is a pilgrimage. It's not that some are religious travelers, while the rest of us hang back to see what might unfold in life. We are all pilgrims—every one of us. The human calling is to live the adventure toward greater and greater depth of meaning. A voyage beckons for us at birth and at death. The travel never ceases.

Once I had the opportunity to see the Dalai Lama and hear him share his message of peace. For years I'd found in him something beautiful and compelling, a radiance of divine love that sparked from his life to my own, creating within myself a deeper awareness of God. As he walked out on the stage, I witnessed the serenity of his face and the surprising energy of his smile. His eyes and smile shone with joy as he reflected more of a sense of humor than I ever would have imagined from such a holy man. I saw his traditional long robe flowing with resplendent colors of deep burgundy and gold. Just to see him was to be in the presence of a religious pilgrim.

Yet, as I looked around at the people seated in the auditorium, I could not help but believe that all of us in that place were also pilgrims. Pilgrimage brought us together that day. People traveling, hungry, thirsty, longing to know our place in this world. People of different races and religions and denominations. And just as the planet is perpetually spinning though we don't feel the motion of it, it is true that we are all pilgrims though we may not always feel ourselves to be on the journey.

My trip to Amherst was a pilgrimage. Perhaps it doesn't compare to the Tibetan pilgrimages of the Dalai Lama, but isn't it also true that some thread holds the two of us together in some rich tapestry of spiritual longing? And isn't it also true that any time we undertake the ritual pilgrimage or enact the family tradition or carry the talisman or keepsake with special fondness, that we share in the deeply human endeavor of seeking God? The answer is surely yes.

Rituals, whether big or small, ancient or spontaneous, personal or collective, conscious or unconscious, call for us to attend to our spiritual journey. They are touchstones for our deepest, most intense, most satisfied existence. They call us both to home and to journey. Home to ourselves. The journey to God.

Chapter 4

Art: The Chalice of Transcendence

Sometimes the juxtaposition of experience becomes more important than the experience itself. In one day I found myself in the presence of art—twice. And that day continues to linger within me in both its beauty and meaning.

I was visiting my friend Dale Martlage in Saratoga, California. We went out for breakfast to a little cafe called the Great Bear and enjoyed the strong coffee, extraordinary pesto omelets, and the pungent taste of sourdough toast. As usual, our conversation sparkled as it jumped between topics both serious and frivolous, ridiculous and sublime.

On the way back to the house, driving down Highway 9, I saw a sign that read *Villa Montalvo*. I asked Dale, "What's Villa Montalvo?"

As I sped past the entrance he told me to turn around because he wanted me to see it. He started to explain that this mansion had been built as a governor's vacation home many years ago, that it once was used for grand bacchanal parties out on the lawn, a place of retreat in the gentle mountains south of San Francisco. In recent years, however, it had been transformed into a lovely place for outdoor concerts. As we drove up the narrow lane toward the mansion, I could smell the eucalyptus and pine hanging in the air. The grounds were perfectly landscaped with flowers and trees. We parked the car and started walking.

We walked around the house, observing the interesting blend of Spanish and American architecture, noticing the large windows and doors opening up to the front lawn that sloped away from the impressive building. As we walked behind the mansion, we found ourselves next to the stage. The mountains had created a natural amphitheatre. There were seats climbing up the hillside, but I also could imagine people sitting out on their blankets, drinking wine, eating fruit and cheese, and listening to music. On this morning, a solitary grand piano was setting on the stage. A young Asian man was tuning it carefully.

Dale and I talked for another minute or two, and then, from the other side of the stage, a man walked around the corner. He was wearing cream-colored linen trousers, a white shirt, and a tan sweater vest. He had beautiful brown skin. He smiled at the young man working on the piano and asked, "Is it ready?" But as soon as he came around the corner, I poked Dale in the arm and said, "Do you know who that is?" I didn't even give him a chance to respond. I said, "That's Andre Watts." I couldn't believe it. Andre Watts! I had seen him on television, on the cover of recordings, had purchased some of his CDs. Yes, *that* Andre Watts!

And then to our amazement, he walked up to the piano and started to play. We made our way up the steps and found a seat on the back row of the amphitheatre. And there we sat. And listened. Listened in the utter silence of the morning. For nearly an hour, I heard Andre Watts play some of the most beautiful music that I had ever heard in my entire life. Heartbreakingly beautiful music, the kind of music that takes you places in your soul, the kind of music that makes you feel long-forgotten feelings or, even better, allows you to feel what you've never felt before. Every now and then, he would stop and play one of the movements a second time as he prepared for his concert scheduled for that night. But for the most part, I enjoyed this nonstop serendipitous concert with unbroken delight.

The second experience of that day happened in the late afternoon. I drove to San Francisco to meet my wife at the airport. After a long lunch in Tiburon, we drove back to the city to get our room. We stayed at the Fairmont on top of Nob Hill. I decided to take a walk around five o'clock. I crossed the street and found myself heading to Grace Cathedral. I've known of this wonderful church for years, and once even had a chance to meet the rector, Allen Jones, but I had never been inside. The building is impressive. The very architecture of the building lifts one's soul toward God. A wide expanse of steps led me to the set of doors opening into the narthex area.

As I walked inside, I immediately was seized by the beauty and ambience of the place. I love cathedrals anyway, but this particular one captured my imagination. I loved the lines of the roof and the way the windows seemed to climb endlessly along the side of the building. The stained glass jumped with color and meaning. And there was a mystical energy around the chancel that drew me forward, close to the place where the eucharist is shared, the word preached, the closing benediction delivered.

But what touched me most was the presence of God that I felt through the art. Most of it was Christian art, but it was significant art, reverberating with depth and meaning. Religious art has a special burden because most of it, frankly, is awful. Frequently, the didactic message of the artist compromises the artistic integrity of the project. But the art in Grace Cathedral was different. There were statues and tapestries. Banners and paintings. There was even a labyrinth on the floor that I walked as an exercise in spiritual insight and prayer. (You can learn a lot about your life by walking the labyrinth.) Some of the art felt old like the Christian faith itself. Yet, there were also contemporary artistic expressions that reminded me of AIDS victims or war victims or homeless victims. *Hervens*

As I walked out of that great cathedral, I felt my soul was in a new place. I somehow saw the world differently, even myself differently. And that feeling was present because I strangely had felt myself to be at home in that cathedral. Yes, it's appropriately named—*Grace* Cathedral—because it was the surprise of grace that I felt in that place. It's not that I came away with any specific message or new fact of the Christian faith. Besides, I got enough of that in seminary. It was something deeper that touched me while I spent time in that cathedral. Who can explain these small beatific moments of wholeness or homeness, moments when the soul is touched by some numinous quality that defies explanation? All I know is that in this religious place I felt deeply religious, which by the way doesn't necessarily always happen when I'm in a religious place. But it did at Grace Cathedral, and part of that experience was the grace of art.

Both Beyond and Within

In both of these experiences—an impromptu concert at Villa Montalvo and a quiet walk in a Gothic cathedral—I felt called to the eternal now. Both experiences were spiritual. Both experiences were soulful. Both experiences brought me to greater awareness, heightened my sense of aliveness, offered to me the joy of divine presence.

This is the power of art and, therefore, the reason that art is such an important touchstone. It brings us closer to the gift of aliveness God created us to experience. To enjoy art or create art, whether it be music or sculpture or painting or literature, is to participate in the flow of life that fills the universe. After all, the universe itself is a work of art both designed and evolving as a source of pleasure.

God, too –

Art is both beyond and within. That is to say, it comes from and is received in the deepest place of the human soul. It adds depth to the human spirit. It requires something and gives something. In fact, that might be at least one important criterion of art—that it contributes to the depth of human experience.

At the same time, art pushes the soul to experience new vistas and horizons. In this sense, it is beyond us. The imagination is engaged. New feelings are elicited. Feelings of surprise and novelty are brought forth. No wonder singer-songwriter Judy Collins recently said at one of her concerts, "Perhaps art is what will save us all." And, in some sense, she is right. Because what finally saves us is that grace that makes us whole. This is the genius of art and also why it is such a crucial touchstone in our aliveness.

What was so instructive about the juxtaposition of these two artistic moments in that one day in California was the awareness that all art has the power to deepen the spiritual quality of life. Some art, such as in Grace Cathedral, is explicitly religious. There is quality religious poetry, such as the writings of Gerard Manley Hopkins. There is great religious sculpture, such as Michelangelo's David. Other art, however, although not explicitly religious, can be spiritually moving and emotionally enriching. Andre Watts, for instance, doesn't do "Christian music" per se, but his music, nevertheless, has more spiritual power than some of the Christian hymns that have been sung in churches throughout the years. Emily Dickinson didn't write "Christian poetry." Fine. But her poetry has a spiritual capacity and sensibility that can move and inspire every Christian.

Art is a touchstone to spiritual aliveness because both kinds of art are driving toward an expanding vision of life. Art, like the spiritual journey itself, is an adventure that calls forth the deepest of feeling and experience. Sometimes this happens at a visceral level. At other moments, it is presented at a more cerebral level. Regardless, engagement is essential to the artistic moment. The spiritual quest is for a novel and coherent vision of life that affirms that existence matters, that life means something, that it is held together by some harmonic beauty and truth. These are the qualities at the essence of artistic experience.

I would suggest that reading a poem or listening to a piece of music or—as happened to me not long ago at the San Francisco Museum of Modern Art—being in the presence of a Matisse painting can be spiritually illuminating and enlivening. It's not even that I got the "message" from the work of art. Art transcends message. The very rhythmic experience of viewing, listening, or reading becomes a profound spiritual discipline. Ultimacy is engaged. And this ultimacy, often painfully missing from our ordinary lives, is deeply within, while at the same time it calls us beyond what we have been. This is the adventurous, transforming quality of the touchstone of art.

Touched by the Creative Fire

Art is an essential touchstone because of the creativity it offers. Creativity touches the core of what it means to be a human being. Moreover, it thrusts one into the very heart of the universe.

In the Christian tradition, there have been two distinct perspectives on the universe.

One perspective accents the sinfulness or brokenness of the world. Rooted in the story of the fall found in Genesis chapter three, this perspective is suspicious of the world. The world is seen as threatening, forbidding, a place to be avoided. To be spiritual, from this perspective, often means withdrawing from the world. Not surprisingly, people who understand their faith from this perspective typically view the world as the domain of evil. Pleasure is rarely emphasized. Desire is scorned. Self-expression is, at best, tolerated. Driven by such a viewpoint, heavy handed moralism often reigns, reducing spirituality to the avoidance of "bad" behaviors or a lifetime struggle with guilt and shame. Countless numbers of people have felt "not worthy of God." This is such a strange and sad notion to me. I think people are just now beginning to see the tragic implications of a life that presumes spiritual wretchedness as the primary human condition.

There is another tradition, however, that is grounded in the perspective of creation. Rather than starting with Genesis chapter three and the fall of humankind, this perspective begins at the beginning (not a bad idea!) and appreciates the central truth that God created the universe and, therefore, has infused the universe with creative fire, love, and beauty. From this perspective, the world is understood as a gift to be enjoyed. Not exploited, but enjoyed and nurtured, even passed on responsibly to new generations. And the experience of creativity, as opposed to being superfluous to the spiritual life, is one of the most profoundly spiritual moments of connecting with the creative essence of God.

In an interview several years ago, someone asked the novelist Henry Miller, "How would you describe creativity?"

Miller replied, "It's godlike. It's a life-giving thing, instead of a death rhythm people are exhibiting. It's getting out of the mold. It's using the mind, the imagination, the heart, the spirit…things we don't see in daily life. Who shows his heart? Who shows imagination?...Well, it comes from God, to tell the truth."[1]

It is true, I think, that we enter into the experience of God when we enter into the flow of artistic creativity. One of the most unfortunate connotations of art is that it belongs exclusively to the domain of artists. Creative fire has become professionalized. The professionalization of art is deeply unfortunate because it robs our culture of an essential touchstone to radical aliveness. The same also might be said of medicine and the healing of our own bodies, religion and the seeking of our own spiritual truth, law and our appreciation of democracy. There always will be professionals, but professionals don't own the fire!

Most people I've met while leading workshops or teaching classes readily admit, "Oh, I'm not artistic!" And that negative response probably developed for many of us early on in our childhood when we weren't able to draw as well as the student sitting next to us in elementary school. We felt self-conscious, embarrassed. Perhaps, if our teacher was rigid, we were reprimanded and shamed because we didn't draw correctly or color within the lines or, God forbid, we were too messy with the paints. Quickly our brain picked up the message—art is something someone else does. Therefore, rather than seeing art as a spiritual touchstone available to all, we came to the conclusion that it belongs to an elite group of talented and gifted people. Think about that. Art becomes for most children a source of judgment rather than joy.

But the fiery artistic impulse, both to create and to enjoy artistic creation, is available to everyone. Sure, there are professional artists who labor and sacrifice for their careers. There is a world of difference between a Wynton Marsalis who performs music at the highest level and an amateur musician who occasionally sits down and plays the piano on a rainy Saturday morning. But what both have in common is this distinctively human experience of making music, and both experiences are authentic.

I like to write a poem every now and then. My poetry doesn't compare to a Mary Oliver or a Robert Bly. At the same time, I don't write poetry to compare it to those professional poets. My poetry is not about judgment. I don't write poetry to compete with other poets. I don't paint with watercolors to compete with someone else. I don't even work at the art of preaching a sermon or writing a book so that I can climb up the ladder higher than another person. There is something essential in the creative process, so essential that it involves my quest for radical aliveness. It's not artistic professionalism that calls to most of us, but human aliveness.

In her book *The Artist's Way,* Julie Cameron has captured succinctly some of the stop signs we place on our road to creativity. Many of us never get past them. But if we become bold, rediscover a little courage and childlike fire, we can decide that these stop signs actually have been misplaced, that we want to rip them out of the ground, throw them away, and never erect them again. She writes:

Stop telling yourself, "It's too late."

Stop waiting until you make enough money to do something you'd really love to do.

Stop telling yourself, "It's just my ego" whenever you yearn for a more creative life.

Stop telling yourself that dreams don't matter, that they are only dreams and that you should be more sensible.

Stop fearing that your family and friends would think you crazy.

Stop telling yourself that creativity is a luxury and that you should be grateful for what you have.[2]

Do these inner voices sound familiar to you? The impulse to create exists, but the stop signs cause us to hit the brakes, come to a screeching halt, even turn around and go the other direction. But if the spiritual life is an adventure, it is time for each of us to journey forth.

For years I had wanted to paint. I had no talent whatsoever in drawing or painting (you see, I learned the negative message very well), but my soul, of course, didn't know such ego-driven limitations. I thought about taking an art class. This is what we normally do in Western culture. Go to the experts, and learn how to do it right. I've done that my entire life. I would typically get a desire, but I couldn't see it as legitimate until I baptized it in some course at the university.

My life changed, however, when I came across some paintings of Henry Miller. Miller, of course, was a novelist, not a painter. Therefore, like a lot of people, his painting was created on the side of his primary profession. Yet, Miller loved to paint. In fact, one of my favorite quotes from this infamous raconteur is: "Paint as you like, and die happy." Isn't that absolutely wonderful! I think there is so much spiritual courage and joy in that little line. Paint as you like, as you feel, as is already inside you to paint. Paint as the child inside you wants to paint. Paint as you like, and then die happy. The point of painting, at least for Miller, was not to make others happy or to be successful or to win critical acclaim from professional artists. (By the way, all the above happened to Miller, but only serendipitously and never because he had a master career plan he was trying to follow.) He painted as a soulful expression of his creativity.

The creativity that makes us human is essential to this voyage of human discovery we are called to live. If it's not painting, let it be music. If it's not music, let it be pottery. If it's not pottery, let it be writing. If it's not writing, let it be gardening or woodworking or sculpting or singing or cooking. The spiritual quest is fed by the fire of creativity. To reclaim creative expression from the professionals, to make it one's own, can be transforming.

Matthew Fox suggests that the mystical spiritual tradition is related intimately to the artistic experience. He writes,

> Is every artist not a birther of images? Thus, every mystic is an artist and every artist is a mystic…Does the artist not image? Does the artist not return to origins? Does the artist not toy with the "irrational" and entertain the right brain as well as the left? Are not the great mystic-prophets those who lived out their images and created spaces where others could live out theirs? Is it not the artist, whom writer James Joyce calls the "priest of the imagination," who articulates the journeys of depth for the people?[3]

This relationship between the mystic and the artist, however, is not yet another form of professionalism. Just as it would be wrong to think exclusively of professional artists, it would be wrong to think exclusively of professional mystics. The spiritual journey belongs to us all. Fox goes on to point out that, "In the creation tradition, all people are mystics. Mysticism is not elitist; it touches the true self in each one of us. All people are artists as well. All persons are both artist and mystic because all are called to be in touch with the true self, the deep experience that is theirs, and to utter images from silent space."[4]

This is, finally, why artistic experience is a touchstone on the spiritual journey. Art touches the deepest, the truest, the most authentic center of human experience. Even as a fire always burns within the belly of the earth, so artistic quality sparks the most alive dimension of existence in the belly of the soul. From primitive markings upon a cave wall to a Matisse that hangs in the Metropolitan Museum of Art, from a primitive African drumbeat to a Beethoven symphony, from a Mother Goose rhyme to a Homeric epic, art belongs to the human experience. To be in its presence is to be touched by fire.

The Soul Food of Image

Everyone's soul needs food. Nourishment. In fact, one reason the arts are so important is that they become a kind of food for the soul. This particularly is true because the arts feed the soul a powerful nutrient called *image*.

Image is crucial to spiritual aliveness. In image, the language of spiritual aliveness is experienced. In the quest for radical aliveness, the soul is invited to respond, as well as create, images of meaning. In the night we dream in the symbolic language of images—running up staircases, walking past a talking dog, diving into a cool lake, making love to a beautiful woman or man. These are not the literalizations of ordinary life; these are the images of the soul. During the day, the horizons of our lives are stretched through the use of imagination—daydreaming it is sometimes called. But in the dreaming of the day, image feeds the soul significant food.

This isn't to suggest that experience isn't important. It is. In ordinary experience, the divine presence can be felt, and meaning can be discovered. Daily moments in life often become the little sacraments of the human journey. Furthermore, intellectual ideas are an indispensable component to the spiritual life. The soul needs ideas of truth and beauty and meaning in order to be sustained the way an arch moves from one end to the other without a hint of collapse. One challenge in American culture right now is that there seems to be a neglect of meaningful ideas with enough intellectual weight to be felt in the depth of our existence. Our obsession with *lite* instead of *light* has created a pop culture that offers little in the way of life-sustaining intellectual intensity.

Yet, as important as experience and intellectual ideas are, the soul finds its development in the realm of image. Image touches the spiritual life at both a conscious and unconscious level. Mystery surrounds image. Who knows why the soul loves what it loves or why certain images break through or why images rise up within the human psyche like little resurrections?

William Carlos Williams was one of the most significant twentieth-century poets because he understood the soul's hunger for image and the importance of image in art. I remember reading his poem "The Red Wheelbarrow" in high school and thinking to myself, "That's strange. It's just about a wheelbarrow. What's the big deal?" Ah, but it is a big deal, because the artistic contemplation of image, the openness to the experience of image, the engagement of image becomes a moment of aliveness. Williams uses images such as rainwater dripping on a red wheelbarrow, images of white chickens, images of the glaze of water.[5]

The words themselves drop like rainwater upon the page. A simple, ordinary object—a red wheelbarrow—an icon of beauty and grace. Suddenly an often-ignored piece of human design, left out back by the chicken coop, forgotten until a little dirt needs to be moved, becomes a moment of contemplation. A wheelbarrow! I read the poem again. Several times. The wheelbarrow starts feeling alive. It takes on an independent quality now. Is there some deep, hidden meaning to the wheelbarrow? Maybe. But maybe not. Maybe the wheelbarrow means only what it means, a wheelbarrow. But it now becomes image, and that image feeds my soul. "So much depends," Williams writes, but what is it that depends?

So much depends... Yes, but what is it that depends? What weight, what meaning now rest upon this wheelbarrow? Could it be that it is image itself? Could it be that a human essence is dependent upon the image? That the soul needs image the way the body needs bread and water and oxygen?

Back in the little town of Amherst, I walked around that traditional colonial house, and all the time I was remembering Emily Dickinson's images.

Image—*I can wade Grief /Whole Pools of it.*

Image—*I felt a Funeral, in my Brain.*

Image—*I heard a Fly buzz—when I died.*

Of course *so much depends*, because what depends upon image is the very development of human consciousness, this coming to life through artistic contemplation. Art gives us image, and image gives us our soul. It doesn't have to be a wheelbarrow. It could be a haystack that Van Gogh painted while living in Arles. It could be a photograph of a pepper that Edward Weston captured while working in Carmel. It could be enormous red dancers floating upon a green canvas by Matisse. It could be the stunning cross that hangs in the sanctuary of University Christian Church in Fort Worth. It could be the elusive butterfly that lands at the end of James Agee's novel *A Death in the Family*. It could be a sculpture by Constantin Brancusi. It could be the haunting cinematography in the movie *The Piano*, with a large solitary shipping crate sitting upon an empty ocean beach in New Zealand. Images become in our minds like animal tracks in winter snow.

Jesus used the image of yeast to talk about the dynamic nature of God's working in the world. Unknowingly, his image of yeast becomes an image of image. It works quietly. Steadily. Yeast does inner work. Like stories, images invite our entrance. But what they finally produce—and what is so needed in our lives—is bread. This bread feeds the soul.

Invitation to Mystery

Another reason that art is such an important touchstone is that it invites mystery. By mystery, I do not mean non-sense. A lot of non-sense out there masquerades as religion or New Age or metaphysical insight. For me at least, mystery is being in the presence of the Divine, experienced often as meaning, as love, as value. Numinous mystery can be wildly ecstatic or quietly ordinary. Mystery can be invoked, but never controlled. Mystery can be subtle or outrageous. Mystery embraces both yes and no, yin and yang, divine and human, masculine and feminine. In mystery, the human soul finds both home and journey. In mystery, the participant discovers both gift and quest.

Art is essential because, unlike so many of our flat, one-dimensional experiences in life, it invites mystery. Mystery means depth, and depth means aliveness.

The mystery that is infused into art is true in both its creation and reception. In the creation of art there is, of course, hard work and expertise, but there also is the more elusive quality of inspiration and genius. Inspiration means that some breath is blowing through the artist. Interesting, isn't it? A breath is breathing through another human being in the act of painting or designing or writing. It is this other breath, the breath beyond our own breath, that is the experience of pure mystery. This is another reason why artistic expression should not be surrendered to the professionals. To have some breath spiriting through our lives is part of our touch of mystery.

What is the artistic expression you need to find? Is it painting or writing? Is it gardening or dancing? Is it woodworking or singing? Is it pottery or poetry? If there is not some art in your life that you are pursuing, you probably are missing this quality of divine breath being breathed through your body.

Margaret is a good friend of mine, and she loves to sing. Although she has never sung professionally, she has voice training that reaches back to her high school and college years. A few years ago she went through a particularly difficult time. She had changed jobs. Moved to a new city. Had just completed a rigorous training program at a hospital.

We were talking one day, and I asked her, "What's the best thing you've done for your life lately?"

She said, "I realized a few months ago that it had been two years since I had sung. I'm working with a voice coach for the first time in years, and I love it. Now I sing just for me!"

For Margaret, the loss of not singing for two years was tantamount to a loss of mystery. She had missed the breath. Part of our aliveness is letting a breath come through us.

The poet Kabir writes: "So plunge into the truth, find out who the Teacher is, Believe in the Great Sound!"[6] How's that for participation? The great sound is the great music, the great breath, the great mystery that comes home to us when we risk the moment of artistic creativity. If we can let such joy begin to flow through us, that flow becomes a touchstone to the aliveness we're designed to experience.

There is mystery, also, in the reception of art. I recently had a chance to see the Bernardo Bertolucci movie *Stealing Beauty*. Although definitely not for the prudish, this film is a lovely and often moving film about growing up, about friendship and families, about the infidelities and truths that hold our lives together. What I like about the movie, in addition to the sheer beauty of the cinematography filmed in Tuscany, is that the movie holds in tension certain ambiguities.

A man discovers that the young girl he is painting for a portrait is actually his daughter from a brief affair years earlier. A young girl, so eager for her first sexual experience, finds that the most handsome boy she thinks she wants actually is lacking in fundamental character and quality. In her quest for young men, it is an older dying man played by Jeremy Irons who becomes her teacher and dearest friend. The older woman of the household, who has lived in this created Italian paradise, decides after twenty years that she wants to move to the city of Dublin, where she grew up. As quirky as all of this sounds—and the film is indeed a little quirky—there is truth, beauty, and, at last, mystery in the midst of all the ambiguities.

And that's part of the reason why art is so essential to the human spirit. Unless we can find grace in the midst of ambiguities, we probably will never find grace. I especially felt this at the end of the movie when the young girl, Lucy, finally found in the most unsuspecting and humble young man her first true love. Their love is itself an image of mystery. After all, one of the most mysterious and alive moments in the human experience is when two people reach out in touch toward each other. All one must do is read the Song of Solomon in the Bible to be assured that erotic energy is the territory of the Divine. But the mystery of the movie touches the viewer in an unforgettable way.

In this case at least, art becomes more than entertainment or diversion. It is a moment of mystery and, therefore, a touchstone to greater aliveness. I think the mark of any good film—or, for that matter, all art—is this unmistakable quality of moving us more deeply into life. A superficial movie or a flat, predictable novel may take our mind off our troubles for a few hours—and that's not wholly unprofitable—but it does not bring us into the hall of mystery.

The Path of Community

The importance of relationships and stories as touchstones for radical spiritual aliveness has been stated. But in the experience of art, stories and relationships come together to create a remarkable moment of community.

Art breaks down walls. Art builds bridges. Art opens up new vistas of diverse culture and experience, allowing outsiders to become insiders, spectators to become participants. Part of the exciting reality of our world in recent years has been the emergence of a global village. Yet that global village is created not merely by technology and communication; it is created by sharing the humanizing experience of artistic expression.

American culture, for example, has been shaped deeply by European reality. The music of Bach and Beethoven, the European masters whose works hang in museums all over the world, writers such as Dickens and Joyce, these and more shaped and continue to shape the cultural art scene of the United States.

A criticism of this European influence, however, has become evident. The influence was obviously too male. Where were the experiences of women? Who would tell their story? Why wasn't their creativity shaping an emerging society? Why shouldn't their work hang in the Metropolitan Museum of Art too? The influence was also too European. What about voices of minority cultures? What about tribal art? What about the creativity expressed in the black culture or Asian culture or native cultures? Aren't their music and stories and poems and paintings art too? It's not that European influences should be discarded as useless. That kind of cultural revisionism would be devastating and is completely unnecessary. Instead, the new opportunity is to appreciate the diversity that exists within the realm of the arts and to allow such diversity to create community.

Community needs the art of other cultures because diverse stories help create community. I don't have the experience of filmmaker Spike Lee. His movie *Do the Right Thing* disturbed me, shook me, made me see a part of American experience that I would be more comfortable not seeing. But the fact that it disturbed me is the reason that I needed to see it. I, like most of us, tend to believe that my experience of America is definitive. But it is not definitive. In fact, one of the most dangerous realities of our present world is the tribal narrowness that assumes *my* experience of the world is the *only* experience of the world. Yet my world is not the complete world, not by a long shot. I need to hear the story of the black teenager as it comes to me through the art of Spike Lee. I need to hear the story of the aged as it is told in a movie such as *Driving Miss Daisy*. I need to hear the story of middle-age anxiety found in a Woody Allen movie such as *Hannah and Her Sisters*. I need to feel the complexity of Asian culture portrayed in a movie such as *The Last Emperor.* I need to feel the vulnerability of a child that is offered in a movie such as *Kramer Versus Kramer.*

Whether film or poetry or music, whatever the artistic form, a diversity of cultural stories needs to be told. With the telling of those stories, a greater depth of community is fostered. The many stories make life worth living. The many stories make life rich, full, fecund with possibilities and insights. More than that, the diverse stories we tell through the arts make the world a safer, saner, more peaceable place. What a wonderful night it was to see the Atlanta Olympics come to an end a few years ago with athletes, not sitting down at a table and negotiating differences, but dancing and whirling and gyrating to music in massive celebration. This is one of the powers of art.

Being a gourmand, I have come to appreciate not only the variety of spices that might go into a particular dish, but also the glory of a French cassoulet or a corned beef sandwich from Shapiro's (my favorite Jewish delicatessen) or a Chinese stir-fry or a Japanese sushi delicacy or a wild night of Greek food with bottles of Roditis and lots of flaming cheese. Imagine for a minute how destitute life would be if it were all American hamburgers, hot dogs, and potato chips. It would be awful boredom.

And the same could be said of the arts. Brahms, Beethoven, and Bach are delicious. But so is bop, hip-hop, hot jazz, and cool blues. And the classics of Homer can feed the soul, but so can Eliot and Pound and Williams. Don't forget Mary Oliver, Adrienne Rich, and Elizabeth Bishop. And don't forget Gwendolyn Brooks, Jorge Luis Borges, and Antonio Machado. Diversity of cultural stories feeds the soul nourishment that grows into community.

Several years ago I had a chance to meet Etheridge Knight. Knight was a remarkable black poet who had led a hard life, a difficult life. Yet he was blessed with a huge, compassionate spirit. He served in the military during the Korean War. Like many, he became hooked on methadone. He came back home to Indiana, facing not only recovery from war, but the starting of another war—the war of race that afflicted all black Americans in the early 1960s. He was convicted of armed robbery. Wrong place at the wrong time with the wrong friends. Spent time in the Indiana State Penitentiary.

While in prison, Knight started reading poetry. He struck up a correspondence with Gwendolyn Brooks. He then started to write poetry. Not the poetry of the university, but the poetry of the street—a kind of ordinary jazz style of poetry that sounded the way people talked. Real words. Real inflections. He wrote of prison and hate and race. He wrote about longing and love. He published only a couple of books, but toward the end of his life Knight had become recognized as an artistic treasure.

One night, an evening of appreciation for Etheridge Knight was staged. It would be a fund-raiser really, an opportunity for friends to raise money for Knight's medical bills now that he was dying of cancer. Tickets were sold. Poets from around the country promised to donate reading appearances. We gathered in the old Athenaeum building off Michigan Avenue in Indianapolis.

What I witnessed that night was nothing less than a miracle. Poets from New York to California arrived. Local poets too. Friends of Knight took their turn, one at a time, walking upon the old stage, finding the spotlight, and then offering their readings to the packed house. It was a happening! The energy was amazing. There were tears. Riotous laughter. There was so much love. So much talent. People of all colors were present. Men and women. Old and young. Wealthy and poor. Some famous, such as Robert Bly and Galway Kinnell. Others were unknown local poets who used to hang out with Knight in order to touch and taste his art.

It was a night of unforgettable community. Art had worked its magic. Walls were torn down. Stories were told. Differences were celebrated. And for a moment, for a moment, those of us packed into that old auditorium were one. It became a moment of the peaceable kingdom. Indeed, art had given birth to community.

The Slant of Truth Telling

Art exists for its own sake, and that is good enough. Pleasure needs no justification. I remember turning the corner one Sunday afternoon at the Metropolitan Museum of Art in New York City, and a Jackson Pollack painting exploded across an entire wall. Massive in size, in texture, in color. Splashes of artistic chaos were in my face like an obnoxious talk-show host. The pictures you find in the art history text books just don't do it justice.

I overheard someone ask his companion, "What in the world is *that* trying to say?"

I wanted to interrupt and suggest, "*That* doesn't have to be saying anything. Maybe *that* is saying something. Maybe *that* isn't saying something. Maybe *that* is there for you to experience the texture, the color, the beauty emerging in the midst of chaos. Maybe *that* is pure joy. Maybe you don't have to figure *that* out. Maybe *that* isn't some secret encoded message. Just be present with *that!*"

There is a certain quality to art that is superfluous, excessive, impractical. And that quality should never be lost upon those on the journey toward wholeness. "The road of excess leads to the palace of wisdom," wrote William Blake. Therefore, music by Bach doesn't have to be justified on the basis that it has a good message. The joy of color in that Pollack painting is truth enough, message or no message. The lines of a Brancusi sculpture become joy enough. Analyze if you want, but it's not always necessary.

In fact, the problem with explicitly didactic art is that it runs a real risk of becoming propaganda. Whereas propaganda is driven by the need to get an explicit message across, art is moved more by a universal quality of exploration, imagination, and love. Now, is there such a thing as Christian art or Buddhist art or Jewish art? The answer is yes. In fact, some of the best art in the world is explicitly religious art. And this art often offers explicit messages, providing the participant with both superfluous joy and didactic instruction. But it is never mere message.

My juxtaposed day in California with Andre Watts in the morning and Grace Cathedral in the afternoon is a perfect example of this distinction. Watts' music had no explicit instruction for my faith. Nevertheless, I enjoyed it and appreciated it as a moment of divine grace. On the other hand, the art that fills Grace Cathedral is indeed art. Form, quality, and integrity were all present. But there was also a message in the art—and appropriately so. The themes were obviously religious, obviously Christian, and through their explicitness my faith was awakened and touched. But, and this cannot be overstated, the art never lapsed into propaganda.

This is my general criticism of the proliferation of "Christian" novels, "Christian" poetry, "Christian" music, "Christian" drama. Most of it—not all of it, but most of it—is awful art, devoid of imagination and magic, and simply a veiled use of an art form to get across an explicit message. Having said all of that, I want to come full circle and suggest that one value of the touchstone of art is that it offers a vision of truth, but normally with a delicate slant, normally in subtle tones, and normally caught out of the corner of the eye. There is truth-telling in art. Not doctrinaire material, but a deep kind of truthfulness that resonates with the human spirit.

Perhaps another allusion to a movie would illustrate what I'm talking about. I often allude to movies because in our culture they are so accessible, maybe the most accessible art form now available. The film *Il Postino* is a story about the poet Pablo Neruda and his friendship with a poor, peasant man who delivers mail each day to the famous poet. The young man is both humorously and sympathetically inarticulate. As unpolished as he is unshaven, he fumbles his way through life delivering mail. However, his heart is awakened when he falls in love with a beautiful young woman who works at the local cantina. So in love, yet so at a loss over how to express that love, he awkwardly turns to Neruda and asks for help. For the first time he begins to read poetry, and, in so doing, his life is changed. Ah, the power of art! He reads love poems, talks to Neruda, becomes a faithful friend. Although a love story between the young man and the woman, the film is more about the tenderness of friendship between the old poet and the young man. It is one of the most beautiful films I have ever seen.

But the beauty of the film is accented by a slant of truthfulness that breaks through to my experience. It's not a documentary about Neruda. It's not a documentary on poetry. It's not a documentary on friendship. And it's not even close to being propaganda. But in the experience of the film's truthfulness, I found myself more alive to relationships, more grateful for friendships, more attuned to the spiritual complexities of love and life and the human struggle for authenticity. The film works, not just as pleasure, but also as truth-telling. Is it an explicitly *Christian* film? No. Nor does it pretend to be. But in its truthfulness, I found something mysteriously compatible with, if not confirming of, my faith.

There is a truthfulness in a Toni Morrison novel. There is a truthfulness in a John Updike story. There is a truthfulness in a Van Gogh painting. There is a truthfulness in a W. S. Merwin poem. There is a truthfulness in a Chekhov play. There is a truthfulness in a Beatles song. The truthfulness of art is beyond message. It comes to us as a resonating meaning—transforming life, confirming life, challenging life. Sometimes it shines like direct noonday sun. But more often, the truthfulness of art shines with a certain slant, like the subtle rays of dawn or the gentle rays of dusk.

The Power to Choose

It's become clear to me that as human beings we have marvelous potential for spiritual insight and joy. We're not mere functions of biology. We're not machines. We're more than the mere complexity of chemicals and cells. We're embodied souls—wondrous, beautiful, powerful, and always about the practice of creating our futures. As I have reflected on the power of the arts, I cannot help but feel that it relates to the choices we make in our lives.

Questions confront us—How do we spend our time? What do we do with our creative potentials? What do we do with our capacity to enjoy beauty? How do we stimulate our mind beyond the mere survival of home and career? What is it week after week that receives our energy and revives our passion? And more to the point—Have we become slaves to the glitter of a Las Vegas culture? Have we become indolent in our TV culture? Is our position of recline, remote in hand, flipping through channels of mindless game shows and infomercials the primary symbol of our living? These are questions that confront all of us as we wake in the morning with these burning potentials inside our bodies.

But the power to create—to accentuate potentials and open up new modes of feelings, to grow with new ideas and enjoy a radical level of aliveness—belongs to every human being.

The arts are not just for the artistic. The arts are not just for the wealthy. The arts are not just for the educated. They belong to everyone ready to be engaged as a full participant in the grand drama of human experience. And it is in this sense that the arts are touchstones. We touch them, yet something in them touches us. The reciprocity of aliveness is played out again and again. But the first effort of time and initiative toward the arts must be made. This is the power and possibility of choice.

Aware of running the risk of being too simplistic and even didactic myself, I want to suggest a practical beginning point in discovering this vital touchstone.

Turn off the television. This will help you; this will help your family. It's not that television is bad, it's just that the constant blare of sound and sight finally becomes mindless. Yes, it can be relaxing to watch television. I like to relax with it too. But far too many of us spend night after night in front of the tube. At the end of the evening what has really happened? Has more potential been discovered? Has more aliveness been activated? Has more depth of soul been enjoyed? Has any relationship in the house been improved? Probably not. On the spiritual journey television must become a thoughtful choice, not a mindless habit.

Go to an art experience. By that I mean go to a museum. Go ahead; put your nose right up to a real painting. See the texture. Step back, and see it from a distance. Step forward, and practically touch it with your eyes. Try to figure it out; let go of figuring out, and enjoy the confusion. Be in the presence of the work. Go to a live concert. Forget the CDs for a while. Buy a ticket. If you can't afford a ticket, watch for free live performances. Go to a play. It doesn't have to be a one-hundred-dollar ticket on Broadway. Maybe it's community theater. Maybe a college production. Okay, maybe it's a high school play; that will do. Just go. Go to a poetry reading. Join a book discussion club. Go listen to a lecture. Get up and go to a movie. Whatever it might be, don't just eat dinner, settle down into the recliner, and watch TV the rest of the night.

Find a creative expression for your soul. Let your creativity flow into some art form. There's a soulful quality to the experience of creating that cannot be ignored. Enjoy. Forget about doing it right for a while. Let go of inhibitions. Give it a try. There's a line in one of Steve Martin's movies,

L.A. Story, that states, "Let your mind go, and your body will follow." It is true. For most of us, it is "One of these days," "I've always wanted to do that," or "That sure looks like fun." Don't procrastinate. Your soul needs some artistic expressiveness. A friend of mine recently started taking piano lessons. Here he is, a forty-five-year-old man, and he's taking piano lessons. It is both painstaking and wonderful at the same time. Not long ago, I asked him how the lessons were going, and his answer was perfect. He said, "I now live better since I started taking piano lessons." Of course!

Awaken to the art of daily life. There is a song in the daily sounds of living. Music can be heard in the sound of buses and cars, in the tat-tat-tat-tat of machines working along the highway. There is poetry in the local idiom of people. There are lyrics in the stories told at the checkout line in Kroger. There are colors in the windows of shops. Sculpture in the lines of a building. Art is all around us. To discover it—or to be discovered by it— is a development of spiritual sensitivity that brings aliveness. I sometimes turn the corner and see a street that could be the opening scene of a movie. Crazy? Maybe a little, but then I imagine characters and music and plot lines. It's all there in ordinary life—this beauty, this art that fills the world.

Affirm the creativity of others. I offer this practical suggestion especially to parents. When your children try their hand at the piano, the canvas, the stage, give them your highest affirmation. It takes a lot to put your creativity out there, though children often seem to be less inhibited than others. Too often adults, especially parents who want their children to have perfect results, overcriticize, overcoach, overanalyze. I know parents do this because I did it for years myself! Affirm. Affirm. Affirm. I had a friend who recently published a book of poetry. Truthfully, it probably should have remained in the quiet place of his daily journals, but he felt this strong drive to publish. Although much of the poetry is mediocre at best, I affirm over and over again his courage to give his creativity to others. Strangely, my affirmation of his effort opened my own heart to greater generosity and grace regarding my own writing.

Cathedrals of the Same Spirit

Back to that day in California—an impromptu concert at Villa Montalvo and a visit to Grace Cathedral. I realize that they were both cathedrals of the same spirit of life that I long to experience each day. Secular and sacred are no longer meaningful designations for me. All of life is sacred if it brings the human spirit to life. Anyplace where art deepens the human spirit is a cathedral experience. A cathedral, you will remember, is a chair where a religious figure would speak with authority to people's souls. Regarding art, any artistic experience that speaks to my soul with the authority of soulful authenticity becomes for me a cathedral moment. And just as the stones of a Grace Cathedral lift one's spirit upward and inward in harmonious synchronicity, so also is the experience of art.

Chapter 5

Prayer: Encountering the Divine

Recently I experienced two dreams on two consecutive nights. The thematic connection for me is undeniable. Dreams often have the power of insight and healing. It's important to listen to our dreams. In fact, dreams themselves can become touchstones in our spiritual lives. I have had dreams, some of which were written in journals years ago, and I still pull out the dusty copies and reread them. Dreams have become spiritual companions for me. One mistake people make is that they want to literalize their dreams. This is a mistake, and even as I encourage you to listen to your dreams, I also want to encourage you to avoid literalizing them. The dreams I'm about to relate hold no meaning for me at a literal level, but they do have the power to bring insight to my life through their symbolism, and I think they bring me to the place of spiritual longing and the heart of prayer.

In the first dream, there was a little girl. Her beautiful blonde hair glimmered in the afternoon sunlight. She sat under a tree in a large, open field, the kind of field I could imagine in Kansas. I walked closer to her. As I moved toward the little girl, I could hear her call, "Help me. Help me." It wasn't a cry of desperation, just a persistent, plaintive call of need. I moved closer. When I arrived, I saw that this beautiful little girl was crippled. Her legs were bent, wrapped in old, heavy braces made of metal and leather. She looked up at me with wonderful blue eyes and said, "I've fallen. Will you help me?" End of dream.

89

The next night I had a second dream. I was walking in a park. It was again a beautiful day. As I walked along, I saw a woman in the distance. She continued to move toward me. As she moved closer, I could see that she, too, had blonde hair. Her features were that of an attractive Scandinavian woman. She held out both arms to me, and then we embraced. We kissed passionately, and then she pulled me down to the ground, wanting me to make love to her. As she kissed me, she kept saying the words, "Heal me. Heal me. Heal me." End of dream.

Strange? Well, I suppose all dreams are a little strange, but beyond the strangeness of the dreams is a revelation from which I cannot escape. In both dreams, there is a beautiful girl/woman. Each represents for me an ideal feminine quality of life that would make me a whole person if I could somehow find it and integrate it into my life. For me at least, the beauty of each of the feminine figures is godlike, each of them representing the "divine child," the "inner child," the "golden child" of my soul. Yet, remarkably, each of them is suffering from some fall or neglect. The insight I begin to live with is that the "divine child" within the realm of my soul is somehow wounded, desperate for attention. The wound is not debilitating but in both cases calls out for awareness, love, help, and healing. The pristine quality of each longs to be restored or reconnected.

It's of no small significance that both dreams are set in a garden or pastoral setting. In the first dream, the little girl is calling for help while under a tree. The tree connects heaven and earth, reminding me that the significance of this dream is about my spiritual or religious life. The vertical quality of the dream points me heavenward, as well as rooting me deeply in earthly life. The image of the second dream, making love in a park setting, becomes like Eden, marrying heaven and earth in the ecstasy of love. Remember, Adam and Eve were naked and were not ashamed. The settings of the dreams—green, lush, generative—become ideals for the spiritual life.

But in both the narrative of plot and the setting of dream is a wound. There is some healing that wants to be done. I wake from the dream and wonder about my own soul. What is it within me that longs to be healed, restored, reconnected? What missing piece of divinity have I neglected or overlooked? What part of my psyche is saying—"Heal me" or "Help me"? What lost garden, secret garden, neglected garden needs to be reclaimed? These are some of the deepest, most soulful questions I or anyone else can ever ask. To not ask them is to deny the essence of what it means to be a human being.

The Beginning Place of Prayer

Where is the beginning place of prayer? Is it getting things we want in life? Is it asking for things from God? Is it like sending a spiritual fax to the cosmos, desperately hoping the order will be filled and be filled on time? Where does prayer begin? Maybe it begins with some prescription, some particular order found in a leather-bound copy of the Book of Common Prayer, dusted off for special occasions. Or maybe it comes from some ornate Catholic catechism or from some liturgy we remember from childhood but have long since abandoned as adults. What is at the heart of prayer? Is prayer always words? Is prayer always in a religious service? Is prayer more than a feeling? Where does it begin? Moreover, how do I begin to discover the touchstone of prayer? And what is the relationship of prayer to my spiritual aliveness? What is its essence? What difference does it really make? And most important, how does prayer become a touchstone for aliveness?

I hope to unravel some of those questions in this chapter on prayer, but for a beginning point let me offer the following—*Prayer is any human action or attitude that invites God's healing love to touch the deepest wounds of our lives and the lives of others.* suggests is outside & an awareness of

That we need this in our lives is undeniable. How many of you reading this book right now find yourselves in a troubled, if not turbulent, what's inside relationship? How many have a family situation of anger, hurt, even despair? How many are reading this very sentence and are anxiety-ridden because of work, career, finances? And what about the quiet desperation that creeps into our lives like a virus? I recently read that more than 50 percent of the American population suffers to some degree from depression. This means that depression has become the statistical norm for living. What of that kind of woundedness? No wonder folk/rock/blues singer Van Morrison sings, "We're going to stay 'til we get the healing done."

We need to get the healing done. In fact, I would suggest that everyone has some blonde-headed little girl or some handsome little boy within inner that needs help, that longs to be whole, that longs to have healing for a child wound. In each of us, there is a divine child, but often that child wanders off, gets lost—lost the way people get lost in snowstorms in Minnesota. For that child to finally come back home becomes of ultimate importance. Every one of us has some Eden, some park, some paradise that longs to be discovered, inhabited, celebrated. In her ode to Woodstock years ago, Joni Mitchell sang, "We've got to get ourselves back to the garden." Garden indeed! In prayer we move toward the healing energy of

become aware

God—the essence of which is love and grace—and in that energy we find our wholeness. Until we find such grace and love, there is no wholeness. Restlessness, only restlessness and sickness. We cave in upon ourselves and are haunted by unrequited longing until we find some kind of home with God.

In his recent book *The Soul's Code*, James Hillman argues persuasively for what he calls the "acorn theory." Simply stated, the acorn theory is that every person has a unique drama to be lived upon this earth, and that our life mission is to discover and rediscover this drama again and again. Consequently, the measurement of authenticity is that we live *our* life, not the life of another, but *our* life. In fact, Hillman suggests that the angels, our daimon, even the Divine are watching over us, sometimes protecting, sometimes motivating, sometimes leading so that we may find our original calling. I often find that my acorn calling is discovered in dream life, especially since I have become so adept at shutting it off at a conscious level. Prayer then can become a moment of discovering our original "acorn essence" and, therefore, be one of the most healing experiences of our existence.

Whatever you finally conclude and practice regarding prayer, I would suggest that you at least give this definition a possibility—*Any action or attitude...inviting God's healing love...for our lives and for the lives of others.*

Saying Prayers and Feeling Prayers

Driving down Highway 1 along the rugged coast of Big Sur, California, I'm feeling the kind of anticipation I remember feeling as a child on Christmas morning. I stop by my favorite restaurant, Nepenthe, have a glass of iced tea and a basket of their decadently delicious french fries, and while I'm there I do nothing. I watch the ocean from the large patio where on other occasions I have clumsily joined in the spontaneous event of folk dancing. I smell the fire burning in the open fireplace. The waitress is friendly, but she knows that my solitude is not some curse from which I'm trying to escape—rather it is a gift I'm trying to open. There is surely a difference between loneliness and being alone. Like most people, I have known both. The wild blue jays fly close, wanting a quick fry for a snack.

While there I monitor my experience. I'm feeling joy, happiness. I feel gratitude for being alive. Much like I felt waiting for Jerry and Diane to arrive at my Indiana cabin, I feel wholeness, almost an inexplicable connection with the heart of the universe. The Bible talks about a "peace that passes understanding," and I'm inclined to believe that it's true. What is this peace, this joy, this grace that I feel so deeply? I look over and see a middle-aged couple engaged in a deep conversation. She looks as if she's in pain. Maybe they're breaking up, I don't know. Maybe they've been married for years, but now they have come to the numb moment when they feel nothing. Who knows? But what I know is that I'm here, I'm alive, I'm aware, I'm living deeply in the skin of my own existence. It feels like I'm home.

And as strange as it may sound, the entire experience—the ocean, the food, the solitude, the cool air, the sun, the smoke from the fire—the entire ambient moment feels like a prayer. Yes, a deep, soulful moment of prayer. In his classic book on religion and psychology, *Insearch,* James Hillman has written, "Prayer has been described as an active silence in which one listens acutely for the still small voice, as if prayer were not asking and getting through to God, but becoming so composed that God might come through to me."[1] That's why this moment feels so much like a prayer; I am composed and listening for God. *Mindfulness*

I might become aware of God's presence

I remember a little poem that the Irish poet W. B. Yeats, a man by the way given over to the ravings of the soul, wrote on the occasion of his fiftieth birthday. It too speaks of this soulful listening.

My fiftieth year had come and gone,
I sat, a solitary man,
In a crowded London shop,
An open book and empty cup
On the marble table-top.

While on the shop and street I gazed
My body of a sudden blazed,
And twenty minutes more or less
It seemed so great my happiness,
That I was blessed and could bless.[2]

Marvelous. Absolutely marvelous. For a moment time ceased to be time, and in this peak moment of experience, he had this intense flow of life, a moment of blessing, of gratefulness, a moment when the feeling of thanksgiving bubbled up inside his soul like champagne, and all he could do was revel in the largesse of life. A leper is healed by Jesus, wheels around, dances with joy, and feels the blaze of his own wholeness as never before. Miriam crosses the Red Sea and, suddenly blazing with ecstasy, she sings and dances before all of Israel. I finish my last sip of tea. Pay the waitress. I feel close to God.

Nepenthe, however, is only a stopping place. I hop into my car and continue down the coast. Past the hairpin curves and loose boulders, past breathtaking vistas. I drive past a little gas station that sells everything from maps, sodas, and gas to psychedelic-looking T-shirts, trail mix, and incense, surely a combination of goods found only in California!

Passing this little cultural oasis, I'm aware that I'm getting closer, feeling closer to what I've come for, what I want to experience. I turn left and drive up a mountain. The driveway is narrow, paved, but the sharp incline and turns require my attention. Paying attention is good. How many days have I used television or recreation or food or work to anesthetize myself? But not today. Today my attention is excellent, and surely paying attention is related to prayer.

Thich Nhat Hanh has helped me understand that the beginning of prayer and prayerfulness is paying attention. He writes, "In Buddhism, our effort is to practice mindfulness in each moment—to know what is going on within and all around us. When the Buddha was asked, 'Sir, what do you and your monks practice?' he replied, 'We sit, we talk, and we eat.' The questioner continued, 'But sir, everyone sits, walks, and eats,' and the Buddha told him, 'When we sit, we *know* we are sitting. When we walk, we *know* we are walking. When we eat, we *know* we are eating.'"[3]

The smells, the sights, the brilliantly colored pheasant running across the drive, I experience all of it with a heightened sense of awareness, and that awareness surely is connected to prayerfulness. I'm present in the moment. Enjoying the moment. How many times have you found yourself somewhere else rather than where you really are? You're at work, but not really at work. You're on vacation, but not really on vacation. You're with friends, but not really with friends. The heart becomes distracted. The mind drifts. The eyes of the soul wander. Most of us have become Houdinis of the now.

At the top of the mountain, I park my car in a gravel parking lot. The building is not big and not even particularly attractive. It doesn't matter. I'm happy to be here. Years ago Benedictine monks made a decision to build this monastery. Braving enormous odds of climate and geography, they built this place with sweat and blood, not to mention with prayer. Big Sur kicks people out each and every day. You stay here only if it is in your acorn! My touchstone friend David Steindl-Rast lives here, and I hope that I may be able to say hello to him. But for now I look at my watch and see that it's time to say vespers.

The chapel is small, intimate, beautifully simple. Very different from the majesty of Grace Cathedral in San Francisco. The walls are white. The benches are a light oak. Small windows dot the walls, offering slight glimpses into the courtyard garden available only to the monks. As I sit there and wait in the silence, I'm amused at the contradiction of life. On the one hand, I live in such a busy and demanding world. Meeting after meeting. Speaking engagements. My nose is in a calendar more than in any holy book, including the Bible. Yet here I am in a place of prayer, a place where prayers are said, not just daily, but several times a day. And here I feel at home. At home as at Nepenthe.

The monks quietly enter the space, and we are led in songs and chants; we say prayers. Some of the prayers are from the ancient tradition of Judaism, a prayer from the psalms. Other prayers are said from the ancient Christian tradition, recited by Christians across the ages. Still other prayers are more personal. People say prayers for sick loved ones. A friend having surgery. A prayer is said for a monk away from the monastery. I say a simple prayer myself—"Thank you, God, for letting me be in this place today." Brother David has written that "vespers is the hour that invites peace of heart, which is the reconciling of contradictions within ourselves and around us." I think he's exactly right. Tonight I feel this peace.

I want to suggest that prayer should be understood and experienced as both being prayerful and saying prayers. One is attitude, the other action.—though the action always needs the attitude.

While at Nepenthe I felt a sense of mindfulness, aliveness, gratefulness. This is the territory of prayerfulness. I wasn't saying prayers as such, but I was deeply prayerful because I was living in tune with the goodness and grace of God in the present moment. In this sense, I was receiving the present moment as a gift of grace—not taking it for granted, not unaware of its uniqueness, not numb to its importance. In the present moment, I was in touch with the divine giver who is both in all moments and beyond all moments of time.

The poet Hayden Carruth writes that such moments are "not mystical, nothing occult, just the ordinary improbability that occurs over and over, the stupendousness of life."[4]

I love it—"The stupendousness of life!" It might be a good bumper sticker. "Demand More Stupendousness!" Certainly moments at Nepenthe or alone on a mountain trail or walking the beach at sunset or wherever you have your most alive moments become prayerful moments. I started this book by sharing a story about a winter evening with Jerry and Diane Zehr. The dinner, the conversation, the stoking of logs in the fireplace created a communal moment with God that transcended words. It was prayer. Life stupendousness! Not prayer with words, but prayerfulness of the inner spirit.

Sometimes when people want to begin the spiritual journey—and particularly the experience of prayer—they ask me, "How do I start to pray?" I used to give all kinds of slick answers, gimmicks, and techniques. Go to any bookstore, and you'll see that there is no shortage of books on *how* to pray. Yet I find myself telling people again and again, "Forget about saying prayers. First learn to live. Live alive. Live juicy. Live passionately. Learn how to taste food. Learn how to relish conversation with another human being. Learn the delight of petting your dog. Learn the sheer joy of sweating after a workout. Learn in the challenge of work. Learn in the quiet of your own living room. Learn by lighting a candle and watching the simple dance of the flame. Learn by listening to music. Learn to be present, mindful, alive to the eternal now of the moment."

And I mean those words, not in any way to the denigration of saying prayers—that's essential too—but I'm convinced that the touchstone we desperately need for radical spiritual aliveness is this outlook of prayerfulness. What made Jesus and the Buddha and Moses and Mohammed the great religious leaders they were is not that they mastered some technique. As one jazz musician told me, "The trouble with technique is that you start to believe it really matters!" Technique is not the path to spiritual depth. Spiritual depth is attitude, consciousness, and a profound psychological disposition.

Thomas Merton, who may have known more about prayer than anyone in the twentieth century, recounts a time when he was standing on a street corner in Louisville, Kentucky. There, on the corner of Fourth and Chestnut, Merton had an epiphany, an insight into humanity and God that would change his life forever. His whole outlook on life became a prayer. He saw the beauty and tragedy of human beings, and he also saw the essential quality of God. Now, don't get the wrong idea; Merton wasn't standing on the corner like some obnoxious religious fanatic reciting prayers. What he experienced was an interior awakening of prayerfulness, similar to Yeats's cafe experience, deeply personal, yet all-encompassing.

Having said all of that about prayerfulness, I want to suggest just as strongly that the saying of prayers can become a critical touchstone for people. And that's exactly what I experienced at the monastery during the evening vespers. Sure, I felt a kind of prayerfulness at Nepenthe. At the same time, the saying of those prayers in ritualistic fashion with the monks became a touchstone for my life. In the Catholic Church, the prayers of the hours—vigils, lauds, etc.—can become a kind of routine that provides the spiritual life with structure. For most of us, saying morning prayers or evening prayers would be a great step in our spiritual lives. Even attending weekly worship, less common in our country than it once was, offers a rhyme and reason to the spiritual journey. Prayer is sometimes called a "spiritual discipline," and although that may sound a little off-putting, discipline is important for spiritual awakening.

Saying prayers from our own experience is helpful. Yes, God knows the feeling in our hearts. But saying the concern or joy aloud becomes a practice of mindfulness. I often find that I have certain feelings toward my wife or children, feelings that are good and positive, but if I never articulate those feelings toward them, I never experience those feelings to their fullness. Feelings beg for expression. And it is also true of prayer. When we have feelings or impulses toward God, we need to say them to God.

I also think there is value in using prayers that transcend our personal feelings. Sometimes I don't really know what to pray or how to pray. I find it increasingly helpful to pray words that are part of a larger religious tradition. For example, the most used of all prayers is probably the Lord's Prayer. Never mind that the Lord's Prayer was not given to us directly by Jesus in the form we use today. The prayer still works, and without a doubt it belongs to the tradition of Jesus. Saying the Lord's Prayer can be a deeply moving moment of prayer. Sadly, it can be said in rote and meaningless ways. But when it is said mindfully, the Lord's Prayer can be a touchstone.

The Lord's Prayer has the power to bring about aliveness. That is also true of the Jewish Kaddish. Or the Shema. It is true of what has come to be called the Serenity Prayer. It is true of the prayers of the Rosary. It is true of the prayer of St. Francis that begins, "Lord, make me an instrument of thy peace..." All of these are prayers that at once transcend my personal ramblings, but carry me gently into my personal existence.

There's a scene at the end of the movie *Dead Man Walking* in which Sister Helen Prejean is following down the hall the man who is going to be executed. He is crying. She is crying. The ambiguity of the situation is tense and true. Is the man guilty? Is he innocent? Should there be capital punishment? What about the criminal? What about the victims and their families? These are the questions of the movie. Yet at that moment before the execution, Sister Helen begins reciting the ancient language of prayer. What else could one pray? The saying of this prayer is not some sleek religious answer. It is a prayer that says everything without trying to say too much.

Some religious traditions, I'm afraid, have created the impression that recitation without feeling is not only acceptable but normative. I think that such passionless, thoughtless, really heartless ways of praying are wrong. As a minister I see this at times on Sunday morning when people come to church, arriving as if they were required to punch a religious time clock and then go off to the real world at noon on Sunday. Maybe you are a person who recalls worship as one of the most boring, empty experiences of your life. This is too bad. Religious service begs to be filled with passionate meaning. I was walking past a church recently and asked a friend, "What do you know about that church?" His answer was a resigned, "Oh, you know, just a *typical* church." It's awful when church and worship and prayer are reduced to this place of being "typical." Yet, despite this typical flattening out of prayer, I would urge anyone to rediscover the meaning of reciting prayers, even ancient and arcane prayers, rooted in history and filled with tradition, because to recite them is to enter into a stream of spiritual depth and tradition that can lead to spiritual aliveness.

As simplistic as it may sound, you begin experiencing prayer only when you start saying prayers. Feeling prayers is a pervasive attitude of spiritual aliveness. It is a recognition that all of living is a prayer when lived mindfully and attentively. Tuning in to this kind of prayerfulness is to discover a divine resonance that fills the world. Yet this feeling is not enough. Just as relationships demand feeling and actions, so praying demands the feeling of prayers and the saying of prayers. Saying prayers may mean simply saying aloud our concerns and joys. It may mean using established prayers in a particular religious tradition. It may mean writing our prayers. Some people enjoy writing in a prayer journal each day. It may mean finding a weekly corporate prayer experience in church or synagogue. In the Buddhist tradition, it may mean simply finding time for your sitting. Saying prayers might mean using prayers from other spiritual leaders and writers. A whole spate of prayer books is now available, many of them creative, eclectic, and interesting.

The saying of prayers and the feeling of prayerfulness are two poles of the same experience. Prayerfulness without prayers tends to become private sentimentality. Yet without prayerfulness, the saying of prayers becomes deadly dry and empty. Feeling and saying become a touchstone for healing the deepest wounds within our souls.

Praying and Divine Companionship

One reason that prayer is so important to the human experience is that in prayer we experience the divine companionship of God. The word *companionship* literally means "to eat bread with another."

In both the Jewish faith and the Christian faith, bread is an important symbol. The bread of God that fell from heaven, the manna, provided the necessary sustenance for ancient Jews to survive a journey in the desert. While in the desert they dreamed of a land flowing with milk and honey, and well they should have dreamed, but they could find the strength to dream only on a daily diet of bread. Of course, the bread given to them as a gift of God was more than bread. There is bread, and then there is bread! Think about it like this—we might be able to live without the pleasure of milk and honey, but we don't live without bread! The bread they were fed was God's very presence and companionship. When manna fell, it was a clear sign that they were not alone on their great adventure of faith.

Jesus also alluded to the image of bread. Often he would refer to himself as the bread of God. This was not some braggadocian claim. Rather, it was his way of saying that his presence was to provide something deeply essential and delicious in life. And just as Jews picked up the symbol of bread, using it in the service of the Passover, Christians transformed the symbol of bread and made it into a reminder of the body of Jesus. In both cases, an experience of communion with God's presence was experienced through the breaking of bread. Don't you think it is true that there is some bread that we all want in life?

Carl Jung once wrote that "human beings refuse to live meaningless lives." And by that, Jung meant that the drive toward meaning, toward some bread of wholeness and well-being, would not be turned away. We are not, contrary to Kafka's grotesque bug, less than human. The soul hungers for divine bread. And as strange as it may sound, every slick advertisement found in the *New Yorker* magazine or every billboard that shows the pouting lips of a teenage model standing forlorn in Calvin Klein underwear appeals to our hunger, our spiritual hunger. Saint Augustine wrote centuries ago that "our hearts are restless until they find their rest in God." And I think it is true.

Hanging in my private study at University Christian Church (I like to think of it as my personal hermitage) is a photograph of mystic, monk, and author Thomas Merton. In the photograph, Merton is wearing a black turtleneck sweater. His bald head is gleaming. In the background is a wall of books. In the foreground is a table replete with pungent Gethsemani cheese, a glass of wine, and of course, bread—a crusty, beautiful loaf of bread. Merton has such a content, happy countenance. He looks as if he is radiating the answer to an ancient question. And that would not be far from the truth. The communion of bread on that table is, in a sense, a symbol of Merton's companionship with God.

For many of us, our orientation toward prayer has been a way of getting things from God. If we want something to happen in life, we say a little prayer. If we want to ask a little favor in life, we say a prayer. If we need a break in life to help us get out of a tight spot, we say a little prayer. Sometimes our prayers are frivolous—like praying for our favorite team to win a ball game or praying to get a date with the most beautiful girl on campus or praying for a new red Saab 900 Turbo convertible for Christmas. (You can't blame a guy for trying!)

But as you know, there are more serious prayers uttered from this perspective of getting from God. I sat with a young woman in a hospital waiting room not long ago. The smell of stale coffee filled the air. Her husband, a young man, was taken into the emergency room with chest pains. As she sat there, terrified over her husband's apparent heart attack, I listened to her rehearsal of family health history, her concern over her two sons, stories of how they first met. Yet punctuating the entire conversation were desperate, plaintive cries—"What if…? What if…? What if…?" And I also heard her mutter aloud, "Please, dear God, please, please let him be all right." This was her prayer, and it was offered with the deepest feeling of prayerfulness, the deepest kind of confidence in God. She prayed, and then we waited.

The theology behind most of our prayers assumes a classical theistic understanding of God. Such a viewpoint imagines God being "up there," holding "all power," making decisions to "grant favors" to our requests. The menacing inconsistency of classical theism is that it assumes God has all the power in the universe and that God is ultimately good. The problem is that if God has all the power and God is good, why does God "allow" or "cause" so many bad things to happen in the world—things like a young father with two sons under the age of ten having a heart attack? This nonpluses everyone. Theologians have approached this so-called "problem of evil" in various ways. Yet, the response of most of them is either that God limits God's own power in the world or that the bad things that happen aren't really bad because God's goodness is infinitely above our understanding. Try telling that to those two boys whose dad died in that hospital emergency room.

This classical theological viewpoint turns God into something of a Santa Claus, prayers into little more than Christmas wish lists, and the life of faith into personal performance (have you been naughty or nice?), thus creating anxiety and sickness. I must admit that this is the orientation of prayer that I was given as a child in Sunday school and that I continue to find most adults believing today. Prayer is defined as getting! We may not say it so baldly, but it's true.

Rather than an orientation of getting, I would suggest that praying is really a way of being in relationship with God. Or to follow the metaphor I'm offering, prayer becomes not a way of getting bread from God, but of being in the presence of God, who becomes our bread. And finally, it is this yeasty, crusty, delicious presence of God that can sustain and provide for our essential being in the world.

Let me quote again one of my favorite writers, the articulate and ever-passionate gourmand M. F. K. Fisher: "There is a communion of spirit beyond the body."[5] What she understood about the dining experience, not to be confused with the mere consumption of food, is that an invisible spiritual companionship is shared at table. This is precisely the central meaning of prayer. In prayer, the divine being is praised. In prayer, the heart is expressive of gratitude. In prayer, the human soul finds its home. In prayer, we sit down at the table of God and enjoy divine companionship. And thus find healing. And thus the touchstone of aliveness.

Now, is it wrong to ask for things in prayer? Well, the answer is yes and no. There are prayers that God will *not* answer. If the essential character of God is unconditional love, God cannot violate that fundamental quality. And if it is the case that God is fundamentally companion and friend, that also means God cannot violate the essential quality of that relationship. God, like any good friend, certainly stands beside us, inviting, encouraging, urging us to achieve the highest possibility of fulfillment in any given situation. And such a presence does have an influence on us and on others. The influence is one of mutual relationship and dignity, but it is influence nevertheless.

The truth be told, it is this influence of friendship and companionship that is most meaningful and most lasting. I can require (even threaten) my son, who is now learning to drive an automobile, to practice safe driving skills. Ultimately, however, no threat and no requirement can produce better safety than simply my encouragement and education of safe driving and his agreement that this value is essential for his well-being and the well-being of others. A son cannot be coerced into being a safe driver. The ultimate option is always persuasion. Granted, such an approach is risky. My son might agree or disagree with the importance of safety. He might agree with safety but have a lapse of commitment to it, and that one mistake could cost him his life. He might be committed to safety, but the other person—driving on the wrong side of the street, driving too fast, making the reckless decision to drink and drive, turning away from the call to be a safe driver—could careen head-on into my son's car and seriously injure him. Driving is dangerous. So are all decisions in life. Typically, the more dangerous the decisions, the higher the satisfaction they promise. The philosopher Alfred North Whitehead once said, "It's the business of life to be dangerous." Life is dangerous because freedom is dangerous. Yet without freedom, we are little more than puppets hanging on a divine string, moved here and there, but not really loving others and not really loving God. Such a view of the human experience leaves everyone in a devastatingly lonely position, including God.

Therefore, to suggest that God will "intervene" or "break in" or "disrupt" the natural and meaningful flow of human events is to ask God to violate the essential qualities that make us human beings, namely freedom and choice. And it would violate the essential quality of God, namely love. To be in relationship with the Divine means that all the risks and all the possibilities of relationship exist. Tragedy and beauty always are crouching on the front steps like a pair of old cats. And although I would never want to underestimate the role of tragic events in human experience, it must be said that even tragedy is a sign of the marvelous potential of relationship existing in the cosmos.

But beauty, these moments of beauty when we freely give ourselves to God and God freely invites us to be accepted and loved, become defining experiences for us. In this sense, God is like the divine lover who prepares herself for intimacy—the gown, the perfume, the fresh flowers from the garden, the soft candlelight—freely giving, freely receiving. This is the metaphor for a relational God. Ecstasy has no boundaries. And with this lover God, this companion God, no force is needed. Moreover, force would be totally inappropriate because ultimately love is not forced. Yes, love becomes a force, but love is never forced. Nor is friendship. Nor is companionship. Prayer is the tremulous giving and receiving of mutual presence. So satisfying. So dangerous.

If the beginning point of prayer is not getting something from God, but being in the presence of God, the experience of praying becomes both question and answer. In our prayers we come to God, seeking, longing, asking, but the answer does not come from someplace beyond the praying moment, as if some product is sent to us from a central warehouse. The answer we seek in prayer becomes the presence of God given to us in the moment of praying. This is why as a father I'm grateful that my relationship with my two sons and my daughter is not defined by what they ask for and what I give them. Things do not define those relationships. Instead, what I finally cherish the most is the relationship itself (and I hope they do too)—the experience of being in relationship and sharing meaningful words that contribute to that relationship.

I don't really know what to make of the experiences I've read of people who have had what are sometimes called "near-death experiences," but I find them fascinating nevertheless. In these near-death moments, persons have walked upon the tightrope of this world and the next, flirting with new dimensions of reality—dimensions I feel sure exist in some form or another but remain veiled to my comprehension and explanation. Yet, in almost all the cases about which I have read, people have experienced a light, a light-giving presence associated with God. I find it interesting that these experiences become moments of enlightenment or illumination, qualities associated with all religions. Furthermore, these visions of light almost always have an invitational quality about them. No force. No coercion. But it is a voice that says, "Come. Welcome. It's okay. Enter in."

Isn't it true that at the heart of the universe is invitation and response?

When we pray, we both offer to God our needs and open the door for God to fill those needs. I want to say clearly that it is not wrong to ask God for what we need. It's safe to say that one sign of a healthy relationship with anyone is to be able to articulate to the other person what it is we need. Children do this to parents. Lovers do this with one another. It is important to notice, though, that as we grow up into more mutual relationships, asking for things in a literal sense is gradually replaced by personal understanding and mutual expression of feeling. In other words, turning prayer into asking, asking, asking is a literalization of praying more associated with childishness than with maturity.

Having said that, there are times when we ask God for specific responses, and I think there is a way of doing that without literalizing the response of God and without turning God into a divine mail-order shopping operation. From my own experience, I can say that I find myself praying more and more for specific attitudes to respond to specific situations. I recently performed a funeral service for a woman who unexpectedly had committed suicide. Her friends and family were devastated. No one, absolutely no one saw this coming. When I was driving to the house to visit with the family, I prayed, "Dear God, help me to listen. Help me say the right words. Help me to know what to say and not say. Help me handle the situation." This was my prayer, and in this prayer I obviously was asking for something from God.

Did God answer my prayer? Well, I would say that God *did* answer my prayer. The answer did not consist of being given a divine script, as if God could fax it to me telepathically. Prayer answered in this way clearly would have violated my mutual relationship with God and my authenticity with the suffering family sitting in that living room. Yet I did feel the answer of God. God's presence gave me a sense of calm. In the composing of myself through prayer, I found the presence of God. God helped me to listen authentically. I felt God helping me find the right words to say. Not too many words. Not cheap, Christian-type clichés. Not words of advice. In my praying to God, I felt centered and balanced. Though the situation of this tragedy was throwing everybody into chaos, including my own human feelings, I knew that I was not alone.

I prayed. God answered.

And I am convinced that the answer I received from God was a greater awareness of God, of love, of human suffering, of compassion. I carried those attitudes into that house—not that I didn't possess them previously, but I felt an intense consciousness of them as I met with that family. I don't want to pretend that I responded perfectly to that family. Could someone else have been more effective with them? Maybe. But for whatever reasons, God, the cosmos, the great heart of the universe had brought us together at that moment of tragedy, and through prayer I felt God helping me.

I know that some urge people to "pray specifically." If you want a new job, tell God about the job you want. If you want a husband, pray for the specific man. If you want a new car, ask God for it. Often quoted is the passage in the Bible that says, "Ask and you will receive." I think this kind of literalization of prayer is unfortunate. To turn God into nothing more than a vending machine is to live with a childish faith that discredits God and demeans the depth and complexity belonging to people.

I think there is nothing wrong—in fact, everything right—with praying to God for specific concerns and concrete needs in daily life. I do this all the time. But to literalize the response of God is to make a childish mistake. When I walked up the winding sidewalk of that home, preparing to meet this grieving family, I knew I had received my answer from God. I did not go into that home alone; God was with me, and that presence is always answer enough.

Praying Healing Energy into the World

Prayer is an important touchstone for spiritual life because it so deeply connects us, not only to God, but also to the divine life that lives in all human beings. When we pray for another person, we are opening our soul to experience that person more deeply than ever before, precisely because in the act of praying for others we recognize that they too have had their brokenness and hurt and woundedness. Indeed, the wounded little girl of my dreams isn't me alone. It is my neighbor too. My brother. My sister. And when I engage in praying for another person, I experience the deepest form of human intimacy, namely, a mutual soulfulness requiring of me an authenticity of being human. This quality of being the human being we all can be is what these touchstones are all about; it is also my depth dimension in life that I too frequently ignore.

Certain people have the power to make an impact on our lives, many times without our even knowing it. For me, one such person is named Steve. I first met Steve several years ago. It was early fall, and he happened to call me on the phone, saying, "Someone gave me your name and thought I might be able to talk to you." A few days later he came by my office.

It's not easy for most people just to drop by and talk to a minister. Some clergy are pretty unapproachable. They either are out of touch with their own humanity or seem to require goodness rather than authenticity of people. And to further complicate the situation, there's a lot of negative ministerial baggage out there. Scandal. Distrust. The list goes on and on. But Steve came by, and I could see immediately that his little visit was costing him a great deal of emotional and psychological energy.

I could tell by looking at his face that he had been ill. His skin color was pale. He looked unusually thin, the kind of thinness that indicates a person has been losing weight too fast. He started telling me his story. At first there were only the polite facts. Married. Two children. He wasn't working right now. Had served in the military. Vietnam veteran. Yes, he had been quite ill recently. But as we talked, the trust grew. This is always a miracle in human interaction, this deepening of trust. He continued the story. He said he needed a church right now. He said that he had tried some other churches, but things hadn't really worked. He said he had some unusual circumstances. He said he needed to let me know some things about his personal life. Quietly. Haltingly. He said he had AIDS.

I assured him that I would welcome him into our church. That's one of the strengths of my denomination, the Christian Church (Disciples of Christ). Normally, our churches are open, educated, and welcoming. More than just offering a church welcome, I assured him that I would be his pastor in whatever way he needed.

The weeks that followed were life-changing for both Steve and me. His health rode a roller coaster of well-being and then severe sickness. We met every other week for an hour. Not counseling really, just talking about life, faith. We talked about his mortality and what he wanted to do in his last weeks of life. I remember going out to visit him a week or so before Christmas. He wanted two things at that point. He wanted to live through Christmas to make sure that his kids had a good holiday. He also wanted to be well enough to attend church on Christmas Eve. Thankfully, he rallied enough and was able to have a good Christmas. I'll never forget the feeling I had at the 11:00 p.m. service on Christmas Eve when I saw him come into the sanctuary during the opening hymn. I felt so connected to him at that moment.

Relationships are touchstones, as I've already discussed, and one reason is that in relationships both people are changed. I think I was changed by seeing Steve's courage and honesty about his condition. I think I also saw Steve change. He found in my acceptance something of God's acceptance, an acceptance I don't always practice perfectly, but that I aspire to represent each day. We became for one another the bread of companionship.

Yet something else happened during that fall. I found myself praying for Steve. Aware of his illness, his impending death, I prayed for him daily. And by praying for him, I felt myself sending out to him the best of my hopes and dreams, the best of God's love and grace. More than that, I felt I was sending Steve God's healing energy. God's healing happens in many ways. The healing of which I am speaking is a healing of companionship.

And that's what I was sending to Steve each time I prayed. I sent him the energy of God's companionship. God's partnership. Not the isolation of AIDS. Not the prejudice of AIDS. Not the sheer terror and anxiety and shame of AIDS. But divine companionship.

In the touchstone moment of prayer, I think we send out to the world God's healing energy. Such healing is not the fixing of things, as if life were like a room in which items merely needed to be rearranged. Our existential life is in need of a lot more than rearranging the furniture of our existence! We need a whole new room. A whole new house. What we send out into the world is healing love to touch the wounds—not only of our own soul, but also of the souls of others. I pray for people I don't even know. It doesn't matter. Praying is releasing healing energy into the world. I pray for people on the other side of the world. It's not that I expect the divine chess player to move the pawns and knights and bishops to the places on the board that I prefer. Instead, I send out the energy of love, knowing that love is never wasted in the world and that love is finally what moves people, heals people, brings people to the wholeness they need. One way I now think of prayer is this: *God does not work in the world by intervening action, but by exerting influence.*

In the winter of the next year, Steve died. But I know that he did not die alone. God had "answered" my prayers in the sense that the divine presence had found a home in the wasteland of Steve's last days. Perhaps one way to think of God is like this: In our praying we have the power to transmit the presence of God the way a radio station sends signals out into the world. The sound waves of grace, love, and hope never die. They travel on and on and on, forever touching those who are ready to receive them. Profoundly, therefore, nothing is ever wasted in prayer. Because, finally, no love is ever wasted in the cosmos. Even the unrequited finds a bed in God's heart.

God's healing energy also came into the world in a different way through my relationship with Steve. I found that the more I prayed for him, the more I was able to do for him. This is partly how God answers prayers. Each day that I prayed for Steve, I discovered that I had more "Steve awareness." The whole issue of AIDS and the church also gained greater clarity within me during my months with Steve. I appreciate better than ever the need for a holistic approach to life in light of Steve's illness. I appreciate the power of community acceptance by having been with Steve. I also had a chance to understand better the issues around mortality, dying, the ways people say and don't say good-bye. And although this wasn't the issue with Steve per se, I came to appreciate how important it is for the church to say yes to all victims of AIDS. How many of those victims, gay men especially, need to know of God's grace and acceptance. By praying for Steve each day I came to appreciate that there is so much that marginalizes our lives and demeans, changes, and challenges some of our basic assumptions in life. Many of these issues I already had some intellectual commitment toward, but by knowing Steve and praying for Steve, I learned about myself. Indeed, I found myself becoming more of the person God wants me to be.

When we pray for others, a quiet miracle begins to happen. Yes, we send healing presence to the one we think of, but more personally, we open the door for God to enter our consciousness and expand our horizons of intellectual and psychological life. Brother David Steindl-Rast, whom I've already mentioned as a dear friend, pauses each day at noon and prays for peace. But Brother David readily would tell you that his prayer moves into two directions. It sends peace out into the world. It also opens the door of awareness within him for peace to find a home. This is exactly what I learned from Steve—healing goes outward and inward. The wholeness I need is exactly what I offer to others, but in offering it to others I find it for myself.

Praying and Community

Having said this about sending healing energy into the universe, it becomes clear to me that prayer is a touchstone moment because through it we bring the human community together. When I prayed for Steve during the last winter of his life, I didn't just have awareness of him. It was deeper than that. I felt connected to him. Any barriers of ignorance or prejudice or indifference were broken down, torn down the way a wrecking ball demolishes a building. I felt a unity with him that surely represents the best of humanity. In the same way, when I pray for others—some I know personally, and some who are just names in the newspaper—I feel a sense of unity with them. This brings the world together.

I was at a party recently and, in the midst of cocktail conversation and hors d'oeuvre chatter, began talking to a woman named Martha. She started telling me how she had been part of a mission group that went to Africa last year. They carried over medical supplies, helped people in a church, provided instruction for children. As she talked, I could feel her passion regarding this experience. It was life-changing. She prays for these people daily. She carries them in her heart moment by moment. And what she saw in the depth of their eyes was real gratitude, a Godlike openness to life and love and hope. Remarkably, she had gone there to give to them, but what happened was that she received so much more than she had given.

This is the mystery of global community. When I pray for others, I bring the human family together. Cornel West vividly reminds us in his book *Race Matters* that it's not the case that we have a poverty problem or a black problem or a minority problem. We must begin to think of persons, not merely issues, and to know that the problems of these persons are actually the problems of "fellow citizens." Too easily we think of others as strangers, foreigners, relating to them as if they are aliens. But they are not aliens. This concept of *fellow citizens* comes alive when we pray for the one human family of the world.[6]

In the Christian tradition the idea of the *oikoumene*—or the ecumenical household of God—is a significant one. Primarily, the word ecumenical has been used to describe the essential unity that exists among Christians. However, ecumenical is really inclusive of all peoples of the world. Buddhists. Hindus. Jews. Christians. The list can and should include all the faces that dot this flying spaceship we call planet Earth. The divine reality knows no territory. Nor does God live exclusively in any one neighborhood.

It is safe to say that the future of this planet rests in the hearts and minds of persons who can appreciate and behave in such a way that recognizes we are part of one family, that race and culture, that affluence and poverty, that geography and territory finally are held together by a deeper vision, a vision of one human family. At the beginning of a new century, the world rests in the lap of irony. On the one hand, the world has never been smaller. Technology, communication, and economics at unprecedented speed have turned the world into a global village. Yet, the world seems to be breaking up into territorial conflict and racial war. It seems unthinkable that at this point in history we still have a race problem. An anti-Semitic problem. An anti-gay, anti-lesbian problem. But we do. And in addition to the political and social work that needs to be done, is the powerful touchstone of praying that needs to be engaged.

Thich Nhat Hanh has made the poignant observation in his book *Living Buddha, Living Christ* that "we can send e-mail and faxes anywhere in the world, we have pagers and cellular telephones, and yet in our families and neighborhoods we do not speak to each other."[7] Could it be that the beginning of our speaking *to* one another is the practice of speaking *for* one another, the kind of speaking that becomes our praying for the well-being of others? Jesus encouraged persons to pray for their enemies because he knew that underneath all the conflict in the world is a reality of community that should never be broken. My enemy is not my enemy. My "enemy" is really a sister, a brother in the human family.

Prayers and the Great Silence

The Spanish poet Antonio Machado has a little poem, or at least a fragment of a poem, where he writes of "listening on the rim of the vast silence." [8]

More than a beautiful poem, his words help us arrive at the heart of prayer. What is the relationship between being awake and listening on the vast rim of silence? We normally think of being awake in terms of talking and doing, don't we? Activity. Conversation. Busyness. And we normally think of silence and sleep. When it's quiet, then I can go to sleep.

But Machado understands an important part of the touchstone of prayer—it's only when we're in silence that we can fully be awake. Remember, "the greatest glory to God is a human being fully alive." Being fully alive means being fully in tune with the solitude and silence of our own soul.

Increasingly, for many of us such solitude is difficult to find. Some of us are afraid of our own solitude. We might have to listen to our own feelings, our own intuition, our own calling. James Hillman argues in his book *The Soul's Code* that each person has a calling, a fate, a spiritual destiny; it's "acorn theory." But to discover the gold of our calling requires—yes, requires—solitude. Thomas Merton has made the point in his *New Seeds of Contemplation* that solitude is not running from people or running away from the problems of society. Prayer is never religious escapism. On the contrary, when we move into the silence of prayer, we can become more meaningfully connected to persons and to our most authentic soulfulness.

In this way the solitude of our lives becomes both the act of praying and the answer to our praying. There is an interior prayer of our living that is unceasing—just as there is an ongoing flow of God's presence that moves within us even as a natural spring flows with refreshing water. It is often our busyness and activity that numb us or lull us to sleep. Certainly spiritual passion can be found in activity. I will suggest in the next chapters that both play and work can become touchstone dimensions for our existence. But in prayer we find silence, and in silence we find God.

The worship service I like the most in the liturgical year is Christmas Eve. On the one hand, it is the hardest service in the world in which to preach, thus my ministerial exhaustion mentioned in the Introduction. After all, everyone knows the punch line of the Christmas story. On the other hand, there is something hauntingly beautiful about the quiet, the silence, the solitude of that sacred night. "Silent night, holy night." I come away from that service less afraid of my own solitude. And the reason is that I find at the bottom of my solitude a God who holds me, loves me, accepts me. In the stillness I am moved. In the silence I find words.

Therefore, on Christmas Eve, though a bit sleepy when we finally light candles together at the midnight hour, I also find, amazingly, that I am wide awake. Silence becomes both an alarm clock for my heart and a bed upon which my soul can now rest. Henri Nouwen suggested, "You have to close yourself to the outside world so you can enter your own heart and the heart of God…" And I know from experience that his words are true. I find myself when I take time to pray. I come home to God when I listen to my solitude. What Machado called "listening on the rim of the vast silence" is such an important dimension of becoming a passionate human being that it is hard to overstate it.

I want to encourage you to find your place on the rim of your silence. It's not enough to read about being alive. Not enough to buy one more set of tapes from the latest New Age guru. Finally, we must practice. Do silence. Do contemplation. Do meditation. Do praying. Do monasticism, even if it is only a few minutes each day that you do it. Find the listening place of interior prayer.

I like the words of Brother David in his book *The Music of Silence.* He suggests:

> If we add a little time to the beginning of our day, even if it means getting up fifteen minutes earlier, this contemplative moment in the early morning can enrich our whole day. Don't worry, you're not wasting time. Don't think you are taking time away from something that needs to be done. Without the contemplative dimension, the whole day can slip away into a mad chase, but those few minutes can give it meaning and joy.[9]

Everyone needs a sanctuary. Not merely one we enter for a formal worship service, but one created in the quiet cathedral of the heart. In that place we pause. Come down. Listen. Listen. Listen. We listen upon the rim of our own silence. And in that interior place, the silence heals our deepest wounds and becomes friend to our most desperate loneliness.

Be still. Be still. Be still. The healing we need and the world needs is found in the praying moment. Be still. Be still and pray. Be still. Pray. And wake up to live the gift of your life.

Chapter 6

Play and Work: Balancing the Sacred Rhythms

It's a clear summer day in Chicago. The sun is shimmering off Lake Michigan, and the entire city pulses with life on a Saturday afternoon. Not too hot. Not too humid. The breeze blowing from the lake feels good to the skin. Lake Shore Marina is busy as the rich and successful move their sailboats out of the slips and make their way to the open waters for an afternoon pleasure cruise. A few miles away, children make mad dashes toward a soccer ball while their parents scream words of encouragement. If you drive a few miles north, you can buy a hot dog and watch the Chicago Cubs play baseball at Wrigley Field. At Cog Hill, golfers are stretching their muscles and taking practice swings in preparation for an afternoon tee time. Somewhere in Hyde Park an amateur musician plays a cello for the sheer joy of playing an instrument. A chef from the Parthenon selects prime ingredients at a market while imagining a creative, artistic, even dramatic presentation on a diner's plate for Saturday night.

Play. Unabashed, uninhibited, unencumbered play. Joyful. Spiritual. Passionate. Engaging. Play calls to our lives in ways that transcend mere utilitarian purposes, such as staying in shape or losing weight. Play is more than mere consumption or necessity. Play is inside our bodies, longs for expression, responds to challenge, revels in the delight and exhaustion of the moment. And why not? Our very bodies emerged from a playful moment of sexual ecstasy. Kate Ransohoff has stated that to play is to meet the divine...to be surprised by passion...to jump on a rainbow.

But life is not all play. The alarm clock will go off on Monday morning. The incessant beep-beep-beep-beep will engage the challenge of work. Calls to be made. Classes to be taught. Meetings to be conducted. Deals to be closed. Programs to be implemented. And, yes, sermons to be written! Work, like play, can be intense and joyful and meaningful, but it also can crush the soul, squeeze our humanity like a lemon, leaving us empty and dry and depleted.

Yet, what would life be like without work? It's true that having too much work can be oppressive, but even more dehumanizing is not having enough work, especially not enough work that provides meaning in our existence. Is there something sacred about work? Yes. Is there a relationship between work and play? Yes. Most important, can work and play become essential touchstones for our living? Again, a resounding yes!

My first job was in my grandfather and grandmother's grocery store, A&G Market in Salem, Indiana. I probably started sacking groceries there when I was eight years old. It was a small store, nothing like the big supermarkets that exist today, and what I remember is that I would stand on old, wooden Coca-Cola cases so I could be tall enough to sack the items. Each year, as I grew taller, they would take a case off the elevated stack until, when in junior high school, I was tall enough to stand on the floor and reach the counter on my own.

But that's not the only thing I remember. I remember that my grandparents introduced me to work. Not just work around the house—put your clothes in the hamper, take out the trash, do your homework—but real work. It was my first job. They paid me for my work. I was to show up and start work at a certain time. I would get off work at a certain time. I was given instructions and expectations about work. Work became part of my responsibility. I couldn't just skip out when I felt like it. They were depending on me.

Part of my work was serving a public, all kinds of people who would come into the little store. Old people. Young people. I remember one man, Mr. Nale, who always came in with two unopened cans of beer in each of the pockets of his cardigan sweater. There were people who came into the store with whom my grandpa would talk for a long time. Others would come into the store, and my grandmother knew that they would complain about something. And then there were those people who needed groceries, people who had no money—rich with hard-luck stories, but no money. "I lost my job last week." "My car broke down and the repair bill was out of sight." "The kids sure are hungry." I'll never forget those stories, and I'll never forget how my grandfather would give them a pound of bologna from the meat counter or how my grandmother would write the grocery bill down on a credit slip and tell them, "Just take care of it when you can." It wasn't just work, but the workplace with all its complexity and curiosity that I experienced.

In that workplace I was introduced to quality. Quality is present in both work and play. It's not that the word quality was used by my grandparents. It was more like "You need to do the job right the first time." I was taught that the canned goods go in the sack first, then the light items, and finally on top the lightest items—bread, napkins, toilet paper. I was taught to put the cold items together in the same bag. "This way they'll stay nice and cold in the car," my grandmother would say. When I carried the groceries out to the car, I was told to put them where the customer wanted them—front seat, back seat, in the trunk—that's for the customer to decide. I learned early on that a few of the customers, almost always women, appreciated having help with their groceries and would give me a tip, fifty cents, maybe a dollar. I eagerly would watch for their return to the store week after week.

I also remember learning about the relationship of work and play. There could be a certain playfulness at work, and that's an element of professional life that should never be lost. But it was also the case that after work I could go and play. Play was more fun, more intense, more fulfilling because I had been at work. Having the responsibility of being at work brought to me a sense of aliveness and purpose. But also being able to run out of the store, and join up with my friends for a basketball or baseball game created a wild sense of aliveness too.

When work and play dance together in a balanced and holistic way a sacred rhythm of aliveness is engaged. I was performing a wedding a few years ago, and after the vows, where I normally say, "Let us pray," what came out was, "Let us *play*." Ah, Freud was right! The couple looked at one another and grinned! Without a doubt, they were thinking more about playing than praying. And they should. After all, when we play it becomes like a prayer, a spiritual quest for joy, transcendence, even ecstasy. No wonder former baseball commissioner and Yale president Bart Giamatti once wrote, "In sports some version of immortality is being sought…" I would suggest that it's not just immortality, but a deep hunger for aliveness over against deadness, a hunger for ecstasy and transformation that is sought in our playing. But not our playing alone. We hunger for aliveness and joy and spiritual depth in our work too. That couple I married will also go to work, pursue their careers, seek their promotions. That will become part of their playing/praying together. The experience of work and play calls to our soul and promises not just answers about God, but the very experience of God.

Let's Go Down to the Garden

In the biblical tradition, it all starts in the garden. Eden. Paradise. I love gardens. Formal. Informal. Even an unkept one has a certain attractiveness to it. Gardens call forth both the experience of play and the exertion of work. Just drive down the Salinas Valley in California and see the workers in the strawberry fields and artichoke fields, hunched over day after day picking, cleaning, and packing. Yes, there is a garden economy that requires work.

But gardens also have a superfluous quality to them. Just to see them is to experience playful delight. To see a vineyard is to be struck by the beauty of symmetry. The imagination turns to a deep red Merlot poured into a clear, bulbous wineglass. An apple orchard or an orange grove offers pleasure without that first succulent bite of fruit. The smell of orange blossoms or the beauty of shining apples dotting the green trees offers an experience of incredible joy. The smell of snapdragons in a flower bed brings delight to the soul. The delicate petals of a rose bush, the last drop of morning dew hanging precariously upon the silken canvas of a red petal—the way a spider web stretches from one plant to another—these have an artistry that should never go unnoticed. And though one might cut a rose or harvest the oranges or sell the apples to a consumer at a market, just to be in the garden is enough.

To play is to enter the garden. Not merely for economic reasons, but for the qualities of joy and passion in living. Like a garden, all play requires a *designated place*. Place might be Wrigley Field, with manicured grass and green ivy dripping off the outfield wall, but there is no play without place. Play is the golf course. Play is the chess board, the concert hall, the theater stage. Play is the bedroom, the hotel suite, the room overlooking the ocean. Play is the botanical gardens, the dinner table surrounded by friends and graced with the perfect centerpiece, the soccer field dotted with children running breathlessly.

I would suggest that this playplace, playfield, playground is related to the idea of sacred space. The garden of Eden became a playground in that it was designated with boundaries as a place for Adam and Eve to enjoy. Enjoy what? Enjoy one another, reveling in nakedness, in the playfulness of the human body. But don't forget the sheer enjoyment of orange blossoms and rose petals, flowing water, squawking birds, delicious fruit. Every sound, every smell, every texture becoming a sensual opportunity ultimately to enjoy God within the boundaries of the garden. Interestingly enough, boundaries are created not to diminish, but to intensify human joy.

In addition to the space of play is a designated *set of rules*. Play is not simply running wild any more than a garden is simply plants growing pell-mell alongside the road. Designated space and designated rules within that space create the right situation for the condition of play. A goalpost is erected. Rows are planted. A recipe is followed. Notes dictate the sounds coming from the musician's instrument. Even gardens that are natural in style are well disciplined within the sacred space of the garden. And, like the boundaries of a garden, the rules within the space do not inhibit the hunger for ecstasy; they intensify both the hunger and the satisfaction.

Additionally, play requires a *suspension of disbelief*. It's not exactly that play is make-believe or once-upon-a-time, although in one sense the imagination is given free reign in the experience of play. Play requires that the normal concerns of daily life be put on hold, and for an agreed-upon moment (two twenty-minute halves, eighteen holes of golf, etc.), play becomes the sole focus of experience. Play requires a willingness to surrender to an imaginary experience of joy and life. If, for example, you watch a movie from the *Star Wars* trilogy, all the while saying to yourself, "Oh, that's not true. That didn't happen. That couldn't happen."— then you've already missed the playfulness of seeing the film. Play invites the conscious mind to take a rest. Not in some anti-intellectual way—certainly play also can be ecstasy in an intellectual garden— but this suspension of disbelief calls to us and says, "Can you come out and play?"

Therefore, watching a Chicago Cubs baseball game is not life or death, though some Cubs fans would argue this point. Its place on the spectrum of real life is far different than peace negotiations in the Middle East. Nevertheless, play does have its place. In pursuit of radical spiritual aliveness, the imagination is given its moment, its pleasure, if you will. Therefore, a novel can be read, a movie watched, or a game of chess enjoyed, even while the pain and agony of the real world continue at their normal, frantic pace. I walk past homeless people on my way to see a movie. Should I stop and help them in their need? How can I watch a movie while people are hungry in the streets? Am I living with misplaced priorities? I want to say that not all of life is play. There are times and places for work and service, especially for the homeless. But as human beings, we must have playgrounds, play-rules, play-imagination in order to become really alive.

Finally, any dimension of play has some sense of *goal* or *home*. The baseball player rounding third heads to home. Ah, the sweetness, the delight, the mythic quality of home. It exists within us all. This longing for home, displayed in novel after novel, movie after movie, is also the stuff of play. The player calls checkmate. Home! Pass "go" and collect $200. Almost home. A runner crosses the finish line. She's come home. She comes back to where she started, only different, transformed, exhausted; she crosses the finish line in a state of ecstasy. Home! A golfer finishes a round of golf. Completeness, a coming around, a coming back to home. I think one of the differences between a good movie and a bad movie is that a good movie often brings us back home.

Play brings us back home. But back home to what? Well, I would suggest we come back home to the garden of our divine source. In playful moments, we both lose ourselves and love ourselves by experiencing play zestfully.

One aspect of my friendship with Jerry and Diane is playfulness. Jerry and I have a special connection because we have become, not so much soul mates, but playmates. When we play racquetball, for example, we enter a court. That's our sacred space, our version of a garden of Eden. In that space we contract to discipline our behavior by a set of rules appropriate for the space. So, even though I could tackle him and win the point, that wouldn't be winning at all because it would violate the sacredness of the space and eventually de-intensify our satisfaction of challenge and accomplishment. After we enter the court, we suspend our disbelief. We don't bring the outside world into the court. We play with reckless abandon. The thrill of victory and the agony of defeat don't tell the whole story. It's the flow of energy and competition that feels so enlivening and playful. There are moments on that court when we almost have danced with competitive rhythm. Moving. Anticipating. Flowing. That's the exact word—it's a flow that occurs in play. And when our game is over— and sometimes while in the process of our playing—I feel at home, at home with my childlike playfulness. Doctors tell me that a chemical is released in my body, giving me a sense of being "high" or "euphoric." I believe it!

In play, we come home to God, to our deepest self, and often to others with a feeling of community and relationship. The history of sport is replete with fabled competitors who at the end of the sacred time and place of game actually shook hands, threw arms around one another, and with mutual respect and admiration became lifelong friends. This is the utter positive quality of sport, competition, and play. Play is an invitation to visit the garden of God.

Gardens Take Work Too

Gardens are places of play, but they also become places of work. In the Zen Buddhist tradition is a saying, "Chop wood. Carry water." The idea behind such an expression is that work has a meditative quality to it, and therefore can become a door to enlightenment. Work and play share the same garden because both can renew and refresh living.

Most of us don't think of work in this way. American culture, still experiencing a hangover from the Industrial Revolution, primarily thinks of work as productivity. Getting the job done. Produce. Produce. Produce. And certainly productivity is part of work. To be able to look back at the end of the day and see that so many units were assembled or so many pages written or so many sales calls made can be a source of accomplishment. But it is this dimension of enlightenment that is often missing in our work.

Sometimes I can close my eyes and remember the weight of canned goods in my hand as I placed them in the heavy paper sacks at the grocery store. I can feel the rhythm of sacking item after item in that little grocery store. There was a certain monotony to the work, but the monotony, the repetition of the work, was part of a life structure that became something like a meditation practice. I didn't realize it then, but I was involved in a practice. The word *practice* carries with it the idea of competency, repetition, pride, meaning, and value.

Later in my life I would learn about the repetition of memorizing noun declensions and conjugation charts as I majored in classical languages in college. I would go to empty classrooms at my university and write on the boards. Over and over and over again I would write the nouns, the verbs, the different forms of Greek and Hebrew. It was monotonous. It was work. But the monotony was not a bad experience; it became the meditation of work and, in a certain way, an experience of enlightenment.

Even now, I probably do work that by any stretch of the imagination would be considered various and diverse. No two days are alike, and I highly value the novelty of my work. At the same time, a monotony exists in my career that is not all that different from the assembly-line work at Ford Motor Company. I write a sermon on Wednesday of each week. Next week I will write another sermon. Then I will write yet another one. I'm amazed at how quickly Wednesday arrives. And so it goes, sermon after sermon. I turn on my computer, open a blank file, stare at a blank screen, and struggle to give birth to a first sentence and then a paragraph, hoping that at some moment an inspired flow will begin to happen. Some weeks it feels easy, and I revel in the gift of inspiration.

Other weeks I have to face within myself, not to mention in ancient biblical texts, the complexity of my fears and hurts and wounds, and the work of writing becomes more perspiration than inspiration, almost to the point that it is unbearable. Yet in the habits and monotony of work, I find a structure that brings meaning to my life. The practice itself is a touchstone.

In his book *Life Work*, the poet Donald Hall writes, "Work is my obsession but it is also my devotion."[1] I like that idea of devotion because, although it does not deny the monotonous quality of work (we all get bored!), it understands the spiritual or meditative dimension of working. To call it a devotion is to appreciate the touchstone quality of work—that a spiritual energy exists underneath the skin of daily habits. Something more than mere production of goods—or, in Hall's case, poems—is at the heart of work. It is a deep human aliveness that is present in our labor.

Hall tells the fascinating story of his work with one particular poem, "Another Elegy." Often people think of writing in terms of gift and inspiration. But rarely is writing experienced this way in practical terms. Writing is like vomiting words, going deep, deep within the skill and psyche of the author, finally bringing the words up on a page or screen. Then there is the rewriting, the editing, more rewriting. This is hard, arduous work. No, it's not the same labor that a migrant worker experiences in the Salinas Valley of California picking strawberries or lettuce. But it is hard work nevertheless. Hall comments that it is not uncommon for many of his poems to take years to finish, since he often drafts a poem twenty-five or thirty times. For *"Another Elegy"* he counts, remarkably, more than five hundred drafts! I find that utterly amazing, but highly instructive. To work on a poem with that kind of intensity and attention is nothing less than prayerful devotion.

Is it imaginable to see work as an offering to the Divine? Work as a prayer? One emphasis of the Protestant Reformation led by Martin Luther was that all work, when offered to God, becomes an act of religious devotion. Luther went so far as to say that if a woman doing devoted work—such as going to the barn to milk a cow—would happen to stumble and fall and die, she would be a "martyr for Christ." I'm not sure Luther consulted the woman about this, but the point he is making is that all work—milking a cow, preaching a sermon, running a business, teaching a class—when understood as devotion becomes a spiritually alive offering to God.

Work is also a touchstone when it is understood as a contribution to community. Unfortunately, many of us measure the meaning of work only from a personal perspective. Although I would never want to compromise the need and opportunity for self-discovery in work, there is a dimension of work that transcends the self—either our own fulfillment or economic success.

Community assumes the interrelationship of all things. I will talk about community in another chapter, but in relationship to work I want to suggest that we tend the gardens of our jobs because the well-being of a whole society depends upon the garden. The social web of communities, nations, and world is intricate, possessing both a surprising strength and fragility. But make no mistake, the world is deeply interrelated.

Regarding work, each of us has the capacity to transform work by what it means to us personally. At the same time, our work contributes to a larger whole, and it is in this dimension to the larger community that work also has meaning. The secretary at a large corporation, for example, has the capacity to find personal meaning in her work. She might enjoy her work, derive satisfaction from a completed project, enjoy the people with whom she works. Yet her work is also meaningful because she is part of the web of that corporation, which is part of a web of a city, which is part of a web of a state and so forth.

Corporate leadership is beginning to understand that quality and performance must be holistic and inclusive. In a hospital setting, for example, the old paradigm was that the doctors were infallible, definitely sitting on top of the pyramid of importance, while everyone else played a secondary role. Now administrators, at least the good ones, know that a hospital functions with quality only when the nurses see themselves as part of the whole. And the same could be said for the custodians and the secretaries and the receptionists. Are doctors important? Of course, but their importance is measured only by their relationship with others in the system.

One reason that work is a touchstone is the soulful satisfaction that is produced when people contribute to the total performance of a larger community. When I am part of a team, not only can the team make a larger impact upon society than what I might make individually, but that feeling of team also provides a significant lift to my sense of belonging in this world. Belonging is one of the most powerful needs in the human experience. To belong, to be wanted, to be needed, to be in relationship with others offers the soul a deep feeling of satisfaction. Learning to live with the solitary quality of the soul is essential, but solitude is not isolation.

Therefore, in work, there is meaning when we can deepen our appreciation for the contribution it makes to a larger reality. This works internally, such as in making an organization stronger. But on a broader scale, work contributes to the functioning of the world. Since my childhood I have been fascinated with cities. Occasionally I go through periods in my life when I want to get away from it all—a little cottage out in the country, no telephones, just me, God, and the crickets. But more often than not, I am drawn to cities. I've thought for some time that I would love to live in New York City. It's exciting. Stimulating. It never stops. And I find the intensity in New York thrilling.

One reason that I'm drawn to cities is that I'm fascinated with how they work. Think about it. It is something of a miracle that millions of people can live and work and play on this little island of Manhattan, and the whole operation of city qua city works! But it works only because cab drivers make their contribution, and the firefighters and police officers make their contribution, and waiters and waitresses make their contribution. This whole city works only when chefs and secretaries, executives and street cleaners, actors and bellhops make their unique contributions to the whole fabric of New York. Each bears a personal meaning in his or her individual life, but each also makes a contribution to a grander picture of human experience. Finally, the gardens in which we work and play are communal.

Doubtless, all of us at one time or another question whether we really are making a difference. I have gone through periods in my life when I felt utterly used and useless. But the touchstone quality of work is a reminder that we do make a difference. All people. All professions. All manner of work. We make a difference to the health of society.

I remember reading a story several years ago in Louisville's *Courier-Journal* of a man who had become quite successful in business. His childhood was very difficult. Poor. Grew up in a rough neighborhood. Had little support from his family. When he was near retirement, he returned to his hometown of Louisville, Kentucky. Now quite successful and affluent, he returned because his second-grade teacher was celebrating her ninetieth birthday. He stood up at the party and thanked her for what she had meant to him. Not only did this particular woman teach the children, but when they were hungry, she would give them food, often preparing extras and bringing food from home. When a child had no winter coat, she would somehow manage to find one or two for the neediest of children. This powerful businessman stood up in that nursing home reception room, tears in his eyes, and thanked this woman for her contribution to his life. He also gave her a very nice monetary gift! But more important than any details of the story is this insightful dimension of work—when we work, we make a contribution to others, and that contribution provides meaning for our human experience, often far beyond what any of us can imagine.

It should never be lost on any of us that we do make a difference. How we treat clients or patients, how we wait on customers or provide services plays a vital role in our society. Our measurement of meaning should not be against someone else's contribution; we should be concerned only to make the best contribution that we can make.

It's far too tempting to believe that we can go it alone or that we can rise to a level of affluence somehow exempting us from the laborers who make up the grand picture of society. The Wall Street broker is still dependent on the nurse who administers his medicine when he's ill and in the hospital. The powerful attorney still needs the skill of the mechanic who works on the brakes of her Lexus. The human family is united by the sweat that comes from our brows. A deep appreciation for one another is called for by us all. Mutual respect is a must. Each of us, feet to the ground of our labor, contributes to one another.

Our Quest for Quality

I want you to imagine a boardroom atop a high-rise office building. That's exactly where I was a few years ago when I gathered together a group of business executives. We called the group the Monday Connection. Our purpose was simple. We gathered once a month to ask the question: *Does anything we do on Sunday morning in our church make an impact on how we live on Monday morning in the business world?* Simple, but not so simple.

I remember the discussion on quality this particular day. Almost all the executives were experiencing major changes in their industries. Some were downsizing or, as one female executive liked to put it, "right sizing." Others were wrestling with balance in their work life and family life. One executive was grappling with the whole concept that his work in the insurance industry really could have a spiritual dimension. From the beginning of his career, he had had one goal and one goal only—to be the top salesman in the company.

I asked him, "Where do you derive the most satisfaction in your career?"

To my surprise and the surprise of the whole group, he did not say money. Instead, he paused for the longest time, almost as if the question stumped him for a moment, and then he started to speak.

"I think," he said, "I think that I really love what I do when I know I have delivered exactly the right product to meet the needs of the client. It's like I know just what they want and need, and I know exactly how to help them get there. That's when work is fun!"

I said, "What you're saying is that you thrive on *quality*."

That one word gave permission for others to begin talking. The bankers talked about quality in their work. The health-care consultant talked about the "joy"—her exact word; sounds almost religious!—of meeting with a project team at a hospital and helping them see new options for an extremely challenging business. A CEO of a national moving company talked about helping families at a very stressful and fragile time in their lives, moving from one city to another, and that if his company does a quality job, he actually helps their lives.

I think the soul thirsts for quality. By quality I don't mean some kind of obsessive perfectionism or even some kind of out-of-balance drivenness. Rather, by quality I mean the desire to experience the symmetry of work, of ideas coming together in positive ways, of delivering something of quality that enriches the life of another. The soul feels at home in quality. William Glasser contends that every human being wants to create what he calls a "quality world." His choice of words should not be overlooked. A quality world is not a utopia. Such a place doesn't exist—especially at work! But quality brings together outer and inner worlds, ideas find expression, conceptualities meet implementation, and the communal moment of one person delivering something of himself or herself to another person is performed.

Quality is crucial for two reasons. On the one hand, in the experience of quality we contribute to the larger well-being of community. Persons are enriched when they receive quality, and that's true whether it comes from a skilled surgeon or a skilled auto mechanic. The second reason for quality is that I am enriched when I deliver it to others. It becomes a moment when I both pour myself into the delivery of quality and simultaneously move past the limitations of who I am, embracing a transcendent dimension of human experience that might be called inspiration.

I find this to be true in my work. As the senior minister of University Christian Church, I am tempted daily to cut corners. Pull out an old sermon. Throw a few anecdotes together. Go for the laugh and not the substance in my sermon. It's far too easy to live off past successes. But to succumb to such temptations would be to betray a fundamental opportunity to present quality in each working day of my life. Now, like everyone, my quality is better some days than others. Remember, quality is not perfection. But I know when I have put the right amount of energy into a sermon. I know it. My church knows it. Delivering a sermon is like giving birth. It's hard work. It calls me to dig down into my own psyche, face my own fears, come to terms with my own demons, express my deepest convictions. Yet, when it happens, when quality is genuinely presented, it is almost mystical in its fullness.

Playing for Quality

What I am beginning to see more clearly is that work and play need to be in sacred balance because they share the same inner drive toward quality. In fact, this is why the two touchstones of work and play can never be separated; work and play share this mystical experience of quality. I mention this because with the touchstone of play, a new kind of body is discovered. This is the spiritual or energy body that is every bit as real as our physical body, though not visible and tactile. In his book *The Ultimate Athlete*, George Leonard remarks that "a field of energy exists in and around each human body...the human individual is viewed here as an *energy being*, a center of vibrancy, emanating waves that radiate out through space and time, waves that respond to and interact with myriad other waves. The physical body is seen as one manifestation of the total energy being, coexisting with the energy body. Its reality and importance is in no way denied."[2]

I think this energy body is related to the spiritual quality of play. When engaged in the fun and challenge of play, an energy body emerges, asserting itself with energy, euphoria, and gladness, all qualities of spiritual experience. In the moment with the energy body, we feel alive, aware, tuned-up, and truly into the living of our lives. This is why play is so essential to radical aliveness. Without play, our life becomes flat, like a soft drink that has lost all its effervescence, and that flatness is deadly. Even people with disabilities have discovered their need to play, compete, experience the joy of sport. One of the most exciting and inspiring experiences I've ever witnessed was a Special Olympics. Although the participants, physical bodies might be limited, their energy bodies flex and stretch and shine. Play keeps the human spirit alive.

Several years ago I had a chance to play a round of golf at Cypress Point, a spectacular golf course on the Monterey Peninsula. I can practically replay that day in my mind, shot after shot, hole after hole. I can recall smells, colors, the glow of the entire experience. The intensity of my quality, my awareness, was so complete that I have never felt more alive than I did that day. In my energy body I remember, I feel, I experience, I come to life.

The energy body that radiates wave after wave of human aliveness is related to the idea of *flow*, championed recently by Mihaly Csikszentmihalyi. He writes,

Contrary to what we usually believe, moments like these, the best moments in our lives, are not the passive, receptive, relaxing times—although such experiences can also be enjoyable, if we have worked hard to attain them. The best moments usually occur when a person's body or mind is stretched to its limits in a voluntary effort to accomplish something difficult or worthwhile. Optimal experience is something we can *make* happen.[3]

This is why play and spirituality are so closely related. When we lose ourselves in play the energy body or the flow of optimal experience is engaged. In this state of aliveness, we feel zest and intensity, and are at home with divine energy. This can happen with work. This can happen with play. Our energy body eats at the table of the Divine. Again, I'll quote William Blake, who said, "Energy is eternal delight." Thus, to play fully is to participate in communion with the divine being. No wonder worship begins and ends with a prelude and a postlude. After all, in between is the delight of play. But communion should not be limited to simply bread and wine on Sunday morning. To play is to eat the bread and drink the wine of God's presence wherever it may be found. Therefore, play in some form is essential to the hunger we have for God.

The energy body of play can be found in a variety of places and ways. Unfortunately, in our culture when we think of play, we tend to think first of the professional musician or the professional actor or the professional athlete. As we have turned play into profession and athletics into entertainment, we have missed the great truth of play for our own lives. Just as I mentioned earlier that art has undergone professionalization, so too has play. To play is not to let someone else do it for us, but to find a way to paint, to sing, to run, to compete, to create for ourselves. Our measurement should not be the professional; it should be our unique experience of aliveness.

I've imagined that someday there will be a pill that a golfer could take at the beginning of a round of golf. This pill would cause the body to glow in sweet, ruddy, honey-tan colors during the time of play, but the pill would be activated only by genuine flow and joy within the play experience. At the end of the round, the golfer, rather than looking at the scorecard, would look in the mirror to see if the energy body had been activated. His or her triumph would be to walk into the clubhouse and have everyone admire how beautiful he or she looked! Was there any radical aliveness? Was there any joy? Was there genuine communion with nature, with golf, with fellow golfers, yes, even with God? Did the game elevate awareness and meaning? These are the real questions of energy body play. After the experience of play, the criterion might become, "Ah, how do I look in the mirror—pale and placid or ruddily aglow?"

Sex and the Playground of Intimacy

Play takes on many forms and has a variety of playgrounds, but one which is universally a part of the human experience is sexuality. For some, the linking of sex and spirituality may seem rather strange. Unfortunately, there has come out of the Christian faith a deep hostility toward sex, if not toward everything related to the body. Sexual feelings have been viewed with suspicion. Sexual expression has been sanctioned within strict confines. And, in some quarters, sexuality has been legitimated only for the purpose of procreation, eschewing all experience of fun, joy, and shuddering ecstasy.

I cannot answer all the misconceptions regarding sexuality that have emerged from religious tradition. At the same time, I can state clearly that such hostility toward bodily life is not the complete story when it comes to sexuality. On the contrary, there is great reason to link sexual experience with a touchstone of play. In the moment of sexual ecstasy we are brought to life, made whole, offered a glimpse into what it means to be united with God. Father Andrew Greeley has suggested that one of the most hopeful experiences in life is when one person touches another. I agree. I would make the following affirmations about sexuality and play, all of which can be rooted in religious tradition.

✓ First of all, I affirm the *essential goodness of the human body.* The old idea that the body and mind are split, that somehow the soul is closer to God than the body, that the soul is imprisoned in the body, or that the body must be transcended in order to find God, is just not true. I do believe in the soul energy of human experience, but the embodiment of that energy is not bad, nor is it intrinsically inferior. We love the Divine with our bodies, and the Divine loves and lives within the body. In fact, as suggested earlier, the energy body emerges when the physical body is brought into an arena of play.

The idea of shaming the body has been one of the most pernicious practices to emerge out of the Christian faith. Sometimes that shame has been self-induced. Often an authority figure such as a parent or minister has made us feel ashamed of our bodies. But shaming the body is senseless and rarely effective in curtailing promiscuity. One reason that the sexual revolution of the 1960s hit our nation with such a fury is that the old idea of shaming the body, shaming the feelings of the body, had been baptized and enculturated in American society. These bodies that we have should never be the object of self-loathing or shaming. The bodies that we have, the wonder of an ear, the loveliness of a set of eyes, the delight of fingers, and the drives of our body—such as appetite for food or attraction to a man or woman—are powerfully good and positive capacities for experiential aliveness. The body we have is good.

✓ Second, I affirm that sexual expression is *designed for mutual pleasure and joy*. Not for procreation alone, but for pleasure and joy and bodily happiness. Like the garden itself, there is a pragmatic quality and an aesthetic quality to sexual expression. To limit sex to the pragmatic quality of conception and childbearing is to miss its wonder and complexity. There is a book in the Bible that some have tried to interpret allegorically, but that I think is nothing more that an erotic love story about two lovers. It's called the Song of Solomon. The book opens with the lines:

> Let him kiss me with the kisses of his mouth!
> For your love is better than wine… (1:2)

Furthermore, the book is replete with lines such as:

> O that his left hand were under my head,
>   and that his right hand embraced me! (2:6)

> How beautiful you are, my love,
>   how very beautiful! (4:1a)

> Your two breasts are like two fawns,
>   twins of a gazelle,
>   that feed among the lilies. (4:5)

> Eat, friends, drink,
>   and be drunk with love. (5:1d)

> My beloved has gone down to his garden,
>   to the beds of spices… (6:2a)

Clearly, breathlessly and clearly, there is a biblical-religious tradition that brings together the playfulness of the human body in the garden of sexual experience. Sometimes I rather suspect that this playful quality of sexuality is being lost in our culture. The sheer pressure of keeping career, family, relationships, and personal well-being tuned up and in balance with one another is a never-ending challenge. Two-career couples drop exhausted into bed, living more as inmates than playmates in the garden of eroticism. Additionally, as we have learned more about human sexuality, it seems that sex frequently has become a dead-serious business! At its heart, sexuality was intended to be a playful intimacy.

✓The third affirmation about sexuality I would make is that *in the sexual experienc we seek to touch the Divine.* Yes, in sexuality there is that place of orgasmic delight, but there is also a drive and receptivity toward the Divine that is also present. Our longing for intimacy, belonging, common-union/communion with another human being is part of a deeper longing we have to be connected with the divine presence. Unfortunately, when persons are not aware of this deeper spiritual longing, frequently they move from partner to partner thinking, *Well, this time, this person will be the one!* But the other person is not the one, at least not the one who forever satisfies one's deepest spiritual longing. I've often believed that affairs occur because people are trying to activate their spiritual connection with God. But instead of seeking relationship with God, they move through a rapid succession of romances and affairs.

And that makes perfect sense because, when in the middle of a romance, we feel as alive as we possibly can feel. We both long and belong. We enjoy and delight. We live in our bodies but somehow also transcend them—or, at least, touch something that is transcendent. To fall in love is the most delicious feeling in all the world—a sign that sexuality and erotic feelings are related to God. Often a romance awakens the soul like a spring shower awakens a bed of tulips. Nevertheless, such feelings toward another human being should not be confused with God. Sex is a gift of God, and with it come the erotic qualities that help make us human. But sex is not identical to God.

Therefore, I would place sex in the garden of human play. This is why sexual abuse and sexual violence are so damaging; they violate the fundamental garden of human experience. Thankfully, men and women are able to grow through and past their pain, finding gardens of delight once again. The playfulness of sexuality needs to be nurtured and loved. Revel in the joy of human touch. The carnival of the human body is good. The playfulness of belonging shared by two human beings is good. The sexual dimension of human experience is like a garden. Pick the fruit. Drink the juices. Enjoy the view. And remember, the summarizing remark after the garden story in Genesis was, "They were naked and not ashamed."

The Moveable Feast

There are many playgrounds, but none exceeds for me the joy of food. The movie *Babette's Feast* is the story of a young woman, Babette, who had once been a chef in a Paris restaurant. There she creatively served food in a city where food and wine are experienced with the utmost of playfulness. There is not a better "food city" in the world than Paris. However, because of a series of events, she finds herself exiled in a small coastal village, taken in and cared for by a very strict religious community. The community is rigid. Small. Isolated. Its austere lifestyle, led by two sisters, is bleak and forlorn.

As Babette becomes stronger, she begins helping the community by preparing meals. Before her arrival, the community ate a rather bland diet of soup and bread. Babette, however, begins preparing better food. Tastier food. She is able to take the simple ingredients and, with a chef's magical touch, serve meals that people begin to enjoy.

The denouement of the movie is a great feast that Babette wants to prepare. She is so grateful for the community, for how the people nursed her back to life, that she wants to give something back. Not to be lost is the lesson that aliveness is expressed when we do for others. But she offers the community what she can—a marvelous dinner. For weeks she gathers the best ingredients. Food is shipped from Paris. The freshest herbs and cheeses are selected. The best wine is purchased. Not just a few bottles, but exactly the right wine that will enhance each course of the meal. The entire feast is an expression of culinary extravagance.

The people in the religious community are scared and worried. They have never seen such excess of food and preparation. Before the dinner they secretly meet and make a vow not to enjoy the food too much. They don't want to hurt Babette's feelings. At the same time they feel that to enjoy the food would be a denial of God. Pleasure is suspect. The body is disdained. And, therefore, anything that might bring the body pleasure should be denied, including food.

The time for the feast arrives. The table setting is a work of art. Tablecloths and beautiful dishes. Candles and silver. It is perfect. The guests are seated, fully prepared to resist the pleasure of the feast. Babette begins serving. Wine. Soup. More wine. Salad. Course after course is brought in from the kitchen. Delicacies such as quail and puff pastry, turtle, french truffles, foie gras, pâté. The feast is served and requires the entire evening to finish. If you're not hungry when you see the film, you will be when it's over. It is a feast that could turn even the most resistant diner into a gourmand.

During the feast, however, a miracle begins to happen. People start enjoying the food. You can see it in their eyes, in the smiles that slowly appear on their faces. They slurp and gulp and relish the tastes of each bite and drink. They are surprised. Grace, of course, is always surprising, and that's exactly what they experience, a sacred feast of grace. Suddenly they realize that, yes, God can be found in the disciplined fast, but God also can be found in the playfulness of food. And in the course of the entire evening, each of them becomes more human, more alive, more connected with one another.

Can food really do that for people? I think the answer is a resounding yes! Not only have I seen this in a movie, I have experienced it myself. I can recall meals with friends, preparing food in the kitchen, sharing dinner, dessert, and coffee, and in that context of food I experienced a heightened sense of aliveness. Eucharist is that moment when Christians share bread and wine. In the Jewish faith, Passover is celebrated with family and friends. Yet, in many ways, when people open their hearts around a table together, a religious moment is possible.

Food, like garden space and play space, has both practical and superfluous qualities. We must eat to live. But eating that is reduced to mere consumption of food is not eating at all. Or at least not living. But to carve out space to enjoy the luscious taste of a tall apple, the crisp white bite, the sounding crunch, and the aroma of apple lifting from the fruit is to be alive. Or to take a vegetable such as asparagus (which, by the way, Charles Lamb said inspired "gentle thoughts"), to take such a long, slender, subtle vegetable and braise it with a little olive oil, serve it with just a dash of balsamic vinegar, and let it have its place beside a small piece of grilled salmon: this isn't just consuming food, this is experiencing aliveness.

Someone once asked famed food writer M. F. K. Fisher why she didn't write about war and love and the "real" issues of life. Her answer was simple. She said, "There is a communion of more than bodies when bread is broken and wine is drunk." This is food and play as touchstone. To share a celebration of food is part of the playfulness that makes human beings human. To ignore such, to reduce life to plastic food picked up at a drive-through window, is to become less than we can be. There's almost something immoral about buying Parmesan cheese in a cardboard container when fresh, imported Parmesan can be enjoyed!

Therefore, I encourage people to learn how to enjoy food. It can become a life touchstone. Enjoy cooking. Enjoy wine. That's neither drunkenness nor overindulgence. That's learning about the mystery and complexity of food, drink, and the grace surrounding it. I encourage people to learn how to cook. You don't have to be a gourmet chef to enjoy work in the kitchen. I encourage families to prepare food together. Children especially need to know all that goes into preparing a meal. In fact, slicing vegetables can become something of a meditation. I encourage people to find joy in the market. I know groceries must be bought, and that's rarely exciting. But to take care in buying special ingredients for special people can be in and of itself a joy and delight. Food requires that we pay attention. To experience fully the bon appetit of the moment is to experience life!

Rediscovering the Sporting Life

As I mentioned earlier, play is much broader than sport. Nevertheless, I deeply regret the loss of sport in American culture. It hasn't disappeared completely; it just seems that we continue to confuse entertainment with sport. I think of sport as sharing in the mystery of human play and, thus, in the intensity of aliveness.

Sport, of course, means different things to different people. For some, sport is running in a mini-marathon, for others it might be an intense bridge tournament. Regardless of the sport of choice, it is crucial in the human experience to find a sporting lifestyle, and, given our sedentary habits, to find physical activity in sport is preferable.

Sport is important for many reasons. It first of all takes the body to a new place. In that new place, life flows in—it comes back like the tide that has gone out but comes back to touch the high edges of the beach. My observation as I talk to many young families is that often they feel life is all outgo. They have to work incredibly hard just to keep up. Keep up with a changing career track. Keep up with educational loans. Keep up with two careers. Keep up with children. Keep up with a personal relationship. There is a feeling of being overwhelmed and under-resourced. Such ubiquitous pressure is all the more reason to rediscover the playfulness of sport. I remember hearing psychologist Richard Moss say that "consciousness loves contrast." This expression means, I think, that we grow in our aliveness only when we live with contrasting experiences. Work is good unless life is all work. Play is good unless life is all play. Most find new aliveness with the discovery of sport.

Sport is also important because at the heart of all sport is the mysticism of meaning. Now, that may seem a little odd, but I think it is undeniably true. Again, another movie might demonstrate what I'm saying. In the movie directed and narrated by Robert Redford, *A River Runs Through It,* a story is told about two sons and their father, a Presbyterian minister. For all three of them the sport/play/art of fly-fishing reveals the mysteries of life. Timing. Respect. Patience. Knowledge. Grace. In the sport of fly-fishing, there is a tension between technique and spontaneity, good luck and bad luck, ecstatic joy and heartbreaking disappointment. And to experience the sport fully—not holding back, but throwing yourself fully into the demand of the moment—is to open the door for transformation. Indeed, in the film all three of these men are transformed by the sport.

One unforgettable scene in the movie shows the younger brother casting his line while standing in the middle of a beautiful Montana trout stream, and as he does, his whole body is transformed into a dance with nature and skill and creativity. He spontaneously invents a whole new way of casting, looking like he is being moved by some mystical force beyond human capability. He fishes at a level that is aesthetically beautiful.

Sport holds this transformative possibility. The miraculous is present in the most ordinary of experiences. A golf swing can become a moment of wholeness. The joy of hitting a perfect baseline shot in the club championship is a feeling of being at one with the universe. The fun of fishing and landing that trophy salmon. The ecstasy of high-fives after your team has won a Sunday afternoon softball game becomes memorable, if not unforgettable. This is the joy of sport. No one can explain why this happens, unless it is that the experience of sport calls us home to the garden of human play-space—not really our garden at all, but God's garden.

Sport, unlike our first impressions of it, might then be thought of as a transformative exercise lived in the present, nevertheless rife with the possibilities of the future. Fred Shoemaker, a golf professional in Carmel, California, has helped me understand that one of the most important questions we can ask in sport is—"What kind of future do I want to create for myself?"

In his book *Extraordinary Golf,* Shoemaker describes a time in his life when the sport of golf itself caused him to face his own fears—not just fears on the golf course, but fears and anxieties about his own life. He finally realized that he was being driven more by his anxieties than his hopes. He now encourages his students to discover the wonder and mystery of sport. He says to students, "Having a future that inspires you and gives you possibilities—that literally gives you life—has a tremendous impact on what you are doing at any moment...Creation means calling forth something from nothing. It has nothing to do with your circumstances. Extraordinary people are not bound by their circumstances; they are able to create their lives anew each day. Yet we all have this ability all the time."[4] He doesn't sound much like your typical golf professional, does he?

I think Fred Shoemaker is on to something of immense importance. In sport, we are able to come to life because we have the opportunity to choose between dwelling on past failures ("I missed the last three shots I attempted") or courageously affirming future successes ("There's no reason I can't hit these this time"). But the existential question brought to us in the play of sport is the big question of life each and every day. What kind of person will I choose to be? How will I make a difference? What forces will I allow to influence me? Sport is diversion and fun, but sport is not escapism and frivolity. In the moment of sport, I find my future again and again. This is why we should play as if our life depends on it. It does!

George Plimpton is well known because of his style of participatory journalism, having spent time in the world of professional sports participating in football, hockey, tennis, etc., but doing so out of a love of sport and a passion to communicate to others the insider quality of sport. In his book *The X Factor: A Quest for Excellence*, Plimpton explores a quality often found in sport, though certainly not limited to sport alone. It's the quality that he variously describes as "competitive spirit, the will to win, giving it 110 percent, the hidden spark, Celtic green, Yankee pinstripes (once upon a time), guts, the killer instinct, elan vital…"⁵ What is this quality he mysteriously calls the "X factor"?

When one enters the play-space of sport, something internally in a man or woman's soul is engaged. It might be to beat the game. Games have rules and goals, remember. Or it might be the competition, to beat an opponent or opposing team. The opponent isn't enemy—no enemies on the sacred ground of play. But for a protracted length of time, certainly, it's acceptable to have an opponent. In the engagement and flow of experience, what often is engaged is this willingness to excel and, if the game demands, to defeat an opponent and win. That pocket of energy inside people is what Plimpton calls the X factor.

Some people live with it and naturally bring it to their playgrounds. The president of the company possesses the X factor at work and at play. The outstanding student in the classroom brings her same academic tenacity to the piano lesson or tennis lesson. Others, however, are surprised to find they have developed an X factor, and indeed, part of the beauty of sport is that it is released, more like unleashed, into the world through their participation. More than creativity, the X factor is that will or strength of mind to succeed. Sport becomes the context for its manifestation.

Some might question if the X factor is all that significant for human aliveness. I know some who fear the X factor, identifying it as nothing more than male aggression, dangerous and demeaning to others. But I would want to argue against such an identification. First of all, the X factor transcends gender and age. I know women who live with the X factor. I know five-year-olds who have it, and I know eighty-five-year-olds who have it too. The X factor is not brutal aggression. The truth is, people who often are aggressive and damaging toward others haven't really learned the transformative qualities of sport. The X factor is not brutishness.

The X factor is that dimension of sport that pushes one to excellence and success. And though success can be superficial, there is something deeply satisfying about success. To win a competition is exhilarating. To come in first in a contest creates a feeling of aliveness. To run against the best and set a new record is to experience life at an unprecedented level of joy. All of this convinces me that one reason play is such an important touchstone is that it creates the conditions in which the X factor can be discovered. No longer is the Generation X motto "Whatever!" acceptable. It is élan vital or no vitality at all!

Balance Is Everything

Presently, a quiet revolution is taking place regarding work and play. Many individuals, some driven by concerns for personal health or larger issues of family, are opting to slow down their career tracks. A recent article in *Money* magazine suggested that Americans are not asking what they want next, but what they want most. Finding that balanced center in work and play is not easy. And I must confess that I have not always done well with it myself. Far too many times I have said "yes" to attending meetings or thought I could fit one more appointment into an already overloaded schedule or accepted one more speaking engagement even though I knew it would throw me into overload. I look back on my life and realize that I have had to explain to my children too many times that I wouldn't be able to attend or that I couldn't pick them up, or if I did pick them up, I found myself running routinely late for my appointment with them.

What might a balanced life look like? Well, it might begin with reducing the number of hours one works. The key, however difficult it might be, is not to work harder or faster. The key is to clarify what it is one should be doing in the workplace. This means clarifying purpose. Business guru and author Stephen Covey encourages, cajoles, even demands that people pay the price of defining their central mission in life. Schedules are then created around that purpose and not vice versa. Until people pay the price of defining, redefining, and refining again their central purpose, it will always be more rat race. And as Lily Tomlin once said, "Even if you win the rat race, you're still a rat!"

Some families are making a conscious decision to scale down their lifestyle. Learning to live on less. Finding the joy of simplicity. I have appreciated my friends Chris and Lisa because they intentionally focus their life energy around family. Chris has his career. Lisa works only part-time outside the home. But they have discovered the balance of work and play in a way that makes sense for them. Is there a price to be paid? Yes. Lisa is losing years of contribution to a retirement fund right now. They still have the same old shag carpet that was in the house when they bought it five years ago. Vacations are mostly confined to weekend trips. Nevertheless, they are one of the happiest families I know.

Rick Warren, who is senior minister of Saddleback Community Church in Orange, California, once told a group that every person needs three experiences. "To divert daily. To withdraw weekly. To abandon yearly." I think he's on to something.

To divert daily, I try to exercise. It's amazing how more effective my work is when I find ways to exercise daily. I also try to pray each day. You may be thinking, "Well, sure, you're a minister. You should pray daily." I know I should, but I don't always do it. Too many days I begin with a meeting at seven in the morning, return to my house at ten at night, and in between there has been little or no praying. But when I pray or let myself read for thirty minutes during the day, I find such diversion reduces stress and invites a new flow of spiritual energy to my life.

To withdraw weekly means that there is a time to let go of work. The old Jewish idea of keeping the Sabbath may be one of the most crucial ideas that needs to be discovered in our contemporary culture. In a marvelous book titled *Practicing Our Faith*, Dorothy Bass invites people to consider unwrapping the gift of the Sabbath. Keeping Sabbath historically has meant something different to Jews and Christians. But the underlying mythology of Sabbath is the same. We honor God and restore life to ourselves by each week pausing for worship, rest, and reflection. Sabbath doesn't have to be on a Saturday or Sunday, but it does require intentionally clearing space for the well-being of our lives, as well as honoring a life principle beyond our own strength. Dorothy Bass summarizes it well when she writes, "One day to resist the tyranny of too much or too little work and to celebrate with God and others, remembering thereby who we really are and what is really important. One day that, week after week, anchors a way that makes a difference every day."[6]

The last element of this strategic trilogy suggested by Rick Warren is to abandon annually. Wow! Think of the wild freedom that goes along with actually abandoning something. Many times the ones who are driven the most are the ones who have led an entire life of overachieving, overfunctioning, over-performing. Yet, there is a grace in creatively abandoning work. Again, for my own schedule, I almost always am away from University Church for the month of July. I just flat out leave! When I return there are a few fires to put out. And actually, after a month, some fires have put themselves out. Funny how that works. But I return wanting to be in the pulpit again, missing the people, ready to minister again. Not everyone, I am aware, is able to be gone for that extended period of time. But it's not uncommon for people to accumulate a variety of vacation days in their work situation. I've known some people to brag, usually very insecure men, about "never taking *all* their vacation." Well, I'm suggesting strongly that our effectiveness at work and our joy at play is increased only when artful abandonment is employed.

The Glory of Work and Play

Pablo Picasso once said, "I spent my childhood learning how to be an adult and my adulthood learning how to become a child again." Sure enough, play invites us to be children again, discovering the beauty of exuberance and the inner qualities of meaning found in the sacred gardens of playfulness. Ecstasy awaits. It always awaits. The numbness most of us have settled for is sad and pathetic. Making time and creating space for play are essential for radical spiritual aliveness. Even as a piano teacher urges her students "to play deeply, play deeply into the keys," so each of us has that same opportunity. To play and to play deeply.

And that same depth of experience awaits work too. There is a beauty and dignity of working that beckons to be discovered. The poet Rainer Maria Rilke speaks of "miracles becoming miracles in the clear achievement that is earned." The glory of working and striving and earning, from sacking groceries in a little store to a major executive position with a corporation, should never be overlooked. When my son was twelve, he said to me out of the blue, "You know, Dad, my ideal life is to have someone pay me to be me!" Sounds good to me! It's not always easy to find the balance of work and play, but surely the spiritual adventure of living requires that we attend to the working and playing. To work and play is to touch glory, even God's glory, and that is always glorious.

Chapter 7

Nature: The Cathedral of the Senses

There is something magical about Santa Fe, New Mexico. The air is crisp and clear. The sun shines hard. The mountains rise up from the earth with a complexity and beauty that are unforgettable. And the sunsets, yes, the sunsets play upon the landscape the way a concerto touches the ear, the way brush strokes of color, more color, more color, touch a canvas. Colors change until there is a deep indigo of darkness resting upon the horizon.

I drive north on the old Taos Road. My son Drew is with me, and we have come here to find something in the land, something moving and real and sacred. Not some new thing, but something old and substantial. We drive north to Abiquiu and then past Abiquiu, driving through the high desert with the mountains looming as a kind of mystical presence. Yes, a presence. It's true that sometimes a mountain is just a mountain. But not here. At least not today. These mountains possess a spirit, a feeling, an energy that makes us feel large and small at the same time. I can't quite explain it, but the silence of the day, few cars on the road, the sunlight bearing down in the late morning, and the anticipation of reaching our destination make for a magical moment.

Occasionally I will say, "Look at that!" And there will be painted rock or majestic rock formations or a river meandering through a valley. I utter, "Awesome." I utter, "Unbelievable." I utter, "Amazing." But this landscape is beyond all uttering. Sometimes there is only silence, but the silence sings a song too. Could it be that just being in the presence of these mountains, like the Big Sur coastline, like the monastery I visit, like the cafe of W. B. Yeats, could it be that just being here is a prayer?

We watch the mileage markers along the road, looking for a turnoff into Ghost Ranch. Ghost Ranch is more than twenty thousand acres of pristine wilderness. There is only mountain and sky at Ghost Ranch. A few buildings are there for a retreat center, but they look small, toy-like upon this vast canvas of nature. I spend the afternoon in a house located in a breathtaking canyon. Next to me is the house of Georgia O'Keeffe, famous for her landscape and flower paintings, famous for her fierce solitude, famous for her relationship with photographer Alfred Stieglitz. O'Keeffe painted this canyon again and again, capturing different slants of light and new colors, her brushes breathing out upon canvases the mystery of sky and rock and light. I stand underneath the twin chimney rock towers, and I see them now as spires, simultaneously pointing me upward and inward, pointing me to an experience of awe and wonder and joy.

The great scientist Albert Einstein spoke of belief in the presence of mystery, a presence that is "partly known, partly hidden." I think Einstein was exactly right. There is something mysterious about this place. To say it's "pretty" doesn't begin to capture it. To say it's "nice" trivializes the power of this place. There is something hard and wild here, something that invites and rejects, that speaks and is silent. And it's not the case that it is there. It is more than there. It is here, in here, in the deepest place of the here and now of experience. Have you ever found such a landscape before in your experience?

Annie Dillard started her book *Holy the Firm* with these words: "Every day is a god, and holiness holds forth in time. I worship each god, I praise each day splintered down, splintered down and wrapped in time like a husk, a husk of many colors spreading, at dawn fast over the mountains."[1] I know what she means, feel what she means, in the here and now of New Mexico, nature holding forth rock and hawk and mountain. W. S. Merwin has written that "remoteness is its own secret." Indeed. Even in the hard, raw, remote landscape of New Mexico something in me is fed and nourished, as if a sustaining energy comes out of the ground and into my body. For this reason I call nature a magnificent touchstone. Like relationships, stories, and rituals, nature has a way of helping us find an essential energy for living.

It is the passing of energy that I begin to feel as I live upon the touchstone of this landscape one late afternoon in summer. Off in the distance, how far I can't quite tell, I see clouds moving over the tops of mountains. Dark clouds. Heavy clouds. And then lightning begins flashing. Coming from the hills of southern Indiana, I'm used to storms being right on top of me. But not here. The landscape is so vast and open that I watch the complete storm move south toward Santa Fe. The light keeps changing. Lightning stretches out in the sky, not quick flashes, but almost like a time-lapse photograph, jagged streaks of light flashing against a darkening sky. Scoop after scoop of deep clouds pile on top of one another. I can see the sheets of rain looking like fog because I am so far away. Wind begins to stir in the canyon, and I feel the temperature start to drop. The pungent smells, the rustle of juniper and piñon trees, and the quick movement of a lizard across the soil are all part of the landscape.

A sacred place is any place, any landscape that inspires you, that helps you experience awe and wonder and beauty. It doesn't have to be the mountains of New Mexico. For some, it is the Grand Canyon. For others, including myself, it is the Big Sur coastline in California. Still others love the Bahamas and the crystal clear water. It might be a modest lakeside cottage in the state of Michigan. A sacred landscape is any place where we finally feel at home.

A good friend of mine, Shirley, loves the English countryside. It's not that she just loves going to England. She does, but it's more than that. She finds herself at home in England, deeply connected to the landscape in a spiritual, psychological, and soulful way. She told me about a recent trip to England, describing experiences, places, and landscapes. After hearing her stories, I finally said to her, "Shirley, you know, don't you, that your soul lives in England?" Her eyes welled up with tears, she smiled, and said, "Yes, I know, I know. I knew it the first time I ever visited." How can you explain the phenomenon of a born-and-bred Texan like Shirley having a soul-home in England? It is surely the touchstone of landscape and nature.

In the landscape of nature, we connect to something deep within the human experience. I would never suggest that it is the only way of connecting with spirit, but it is one way—in fact, one very important way of finding God. After years of conducting retreats with people focused on spiritual development, I have learned that one of the most potent questions to ask people is: "What is one of your most spiritual moments?" Invariably, the answers run in the direction of nature. "The mountains." "The ocean." "The desert." These are the three places people most often recount in the telling of their spiritual narrative, and I can only affirm the direction of their responses.

While at Ghost Ranch, I felt feelings of awe, wonder, joy, fascination. I felt isolated, afraid, drawn to something ineffable. I felt small in the vast world. I felt the world large, expansive, full of energy and life. I felt part of a larger pattern of life. I felt part of the unfolding of life. On this very place, dinosaur bones have been excavated. Imagining myself on the same terra firma as dinosaurs was awesome. I was full at this place. My experience as a human being felt rich at this place. I felt impoverished too. Nothing matters in this wilderness except your ability to survive it. The label on your clothes is meaningless in the wilderness. You don't show a mountain your résumé, either. The wilderness is always, forever, ultimately most important. Again, Annie Dillard has written, "This is the one world, bound to itself and exultant."[2] Or, if you prefer, the ancient prophet Isaiah wrote, "The whole earth is full of the glory of God."

And I think in this moment, in this cathedral of nature, a language is being spoken. Why today a thunderstorm? Why the lightning? What message was there for me in the storm? Anything? Everything? Am I over-reading nature? It can be done. Or is there something inside me that needs this touchstone of nature? Alan Watts used to laugh when people would ask him, "Do you believe in heaven?" He always would reply, "Go to outer space and look back at the earth. Where do you think we are?" Is this rock, this soil, these plants, these lizards scurrying under my feet heaven? Have I lived and gone to heaven too? And if not heaven, at the very least, don't these natural realities have something to say about heaven or about what it means to be alive in the heavens?

How is this for a spiritual discipline? Go to the mountains regularly. Visit the ocean and enter the feminine flow of giving and receiving. Find a field in which to walk, a country road to travel, a park in which to sit and smell the air after a spring shower. Do you want to grow spiritually? Go and feel the bark of a tree. Touch the moss with your fingers on the side of the house. As human beings we need nature the way we need God. Maybe God and nature are one. Some suggest this is so. Others suggest that God is radically present in nature. Still others, even the most skeptical, suggest that there is no God, only nature. But inexplicably they nevertheless are moved spiritually by nature, finding in mountains or desert the tremendous mystery of reality. If that is so, if that experience is real for them, that moment is a transcendent experience that becomes God too.

Driving back to Santa Fe I find myself looking forward to dinner at the Coyote Cafe. Ah, that's a touchstone too. But in driving through mountains and mesas, in seeing the awesomeness of this place, I have come to life. A resurrection of sorts. I am changed. What is it that has drawn near? Is it God? Is it some life spirit that is beyond naming? Is it Native American? Is it Christian? Is it Jewish? Is it Buddhist? What is it that has seeped from this landscape into the psychological landscape of my own body?

Are there mountains inside me? And oceans too? And rivers? Are there storms brewing in my body? Lightning? The answer is surely yes.

Inner and Outer Landscapes

Life longs for texture. To touch the hardness of granite rock is to know texture. To feel the soft, scratchy fibers of a wool sweater in our hands or to taste the sharp crunch of celery in our mouths is to experience texture. Without texture, life would be boring and flat, without contrast or interest.

One reason geographical landscape is so important in the human experience is that it has texture. Some texture is dramatic—like a mesa rising from the earth or the ocean crashing wildly against granite rocks. But there are subtle textures to nature—the curve of a plowed field against a gray spring sky, the quiet buzz of a bee moving from flower to flower in a backyard garden, or the grace of a butterfly as it finally lands on the front porch of a house. Texture. There is a spiritual exercise that suggests that if you walk attentively enough, slowly enough, consciously enough, you are able to feel the curve of the earth under your feet. Could this be? This brings mindfulness, prayer, and nature together.

In a spiritual sense, all people have an inner landscape, textures of feeling and ideas that shape life and finally make life worth living. Living with texture means living open to spiritual depth, spiritual complexity, spiritual possibility. Living with texture means openness, awareness, intuneness with our inner life upon the outer landscapes of our lives. If we were all accountants or all teachers or all ministers, the world would be a terribly boring place. But the world is not boring because there is a deep-down texture to life. Texture is living with contrasts. Not everything is light. Not everything is dark. The shadows make life interesting.

I often have met people who defined their religious life almost exclusively in terms of being good. By "good" they most often mean not doing anything wrong. The problem with this approach to life, however, is that they are eliminating texture from the landscape. Instead of living with jagged peaks or wild rivers or exciting oceans, they have reduced themselves to Teflon people—nothing sticks, no friction is present, and usually nothing is felt. To me, religion and spirituality are designed to enhance human experience, not deny it, reduce it, or flatten it out like a flour tortilla. This isn't to suggest that we go out and do things that are destructive just to give our lives texture. It is simply to suggest that for life to have intensity, there must be texture in the entire experience.

I mention this because what nature offers is texture, both in feeling and thought. The poet Robert Bly makes the point in his book *News of the Universe: Poems of Twofold Consciousness* that a poet must live in two stages. The first stage is subjectivity. That's where most poetry begins. Perhaps you have tried to write a poem or two, and my guess is that the poem you wrote started with what you were feeling. We fall in love, and all we can do is write a poem. We feel very sad, and therefore we try to write a poem. One reason poets are so important to our spiritual landscape is that they feel and, therefore, call upon others to rediscover their subjectivity.

However, poets must move on to another stage, as must all radically alive people, moving into a stage characterized by seeing. Many wonderful poems, sometimes called object poems or prose poems, not only describe an object, but also move inside the object and, thus, inside the reader. It's a strange paradox, but the more we can see outwardly, the more we can see and feel inwardly. Seeing is critical to living. A good example of an object poem comes from Bly. Notice how the following poem — one could argue that this is prose and not a poem—invites the reader to see nature. Not to look through it, as if it were a symbol of something, but deeply at and in something. Undoubtedly nature can be a symbol of something, but in the poem, this looking at nature as nature is a complete experience in and of itself.

> Alone on the jagged rock at the south end of McClure's Beach. The sky low. The sea grows more and more private, as afternoon goes on; the sky comes down closer; the unobserved water rushes out to the horizon, horses galloping in a mountain valley at night. The waves smash up the rock; I find flags of seaweed high on the worn top, forty feet up, thrown up overnight separated water still pooled there, like the black ducks that fly desolate, forlorn, and joyful over the seething swells, who never "feel pity for themselves," and "do not lie awake weeping for their sins." In their blood cells the vultures coast with furry necks extended, watching over the desert for signs of life to end. It is not our life we need to weep for. Inside us there is some secret. We are following a narrow ledge around a mountain, we are sailing on skeletal eerie craft over the buoyant ocean.[3]

Obviously Bly is seeing. This act of both experiencing and seeing nature is indispensable in the human quest for inner life. Many of us go through life not seeing. We are either too busy to see or too numb to feel or too distracted to think. The suggestion was made earlier in the book that mindfulness is key, and I believe it is. Coming to life doesn't begin with "five fabulous steps to faith"! There are no steps. Only one step. *Seeing*. No wonder Jesus said to people, "You have eyes, but do not see."

In our seeing, we experience texture and create texture within our lives. Bly's poem has a certain degree of psychological weight to be sure, but it also has a heady sense of texture. It is this texture that makes life worth living, and by finding texture in the outer landscape of the world, we are able to discover it within the inner landscape of our soul. I see New Mexico, and New Mexico is there. But New Mexico is also here, deeply, soulfully, spiritually here. Yet I will never know of the inner mountain, inner ocean, inner wilderness, unless I cultivate a sense of seeing. I don't want to give the impression that one must travel to some exotic place to find the observance of nature. It can happen at the Grand Canyon, of course, or Tibet or England or the Galapagos Islands. But this oneness of landscape can happen on your drive to work or sitting on your deck in your backyard. Nature is the cathedral that never closes.

The Divine Body

How we understand nature, its meaning and intrinsic value, finally is shaped by what we believe to be true of ultimate reality. This is the realm of faith. Faith is not so much intellectual ascent to a creed or belief system as it is an inward way of seeing and experiencing the world. For example, a person who sees the earth as little more than a resource of natural products to be used in the advancement of an economic system will treat the earth in a manner consistent with that viewpoint. I saw an advertisement in the *Boston Globe* a few years ago for a realty company that demonstrated such a crass perspective. There was a photograph of the planet Earth and underneath was the caption, "Planet Earth Is Our Product." I seriously question if Earth is anyone's "product." Nevertheless, that is a viewpoint that has been dominant in the twentieth century.

We now are facing the reality that the planet Earth is in trouble—polluted, exploited, and unable to sustain lifestyles of waste and destruction. Our consumption is outrunning the earth's ability to provide natural resources. Moreover, we just now are beginning to appreciate the radical and delicate web of life that exists in the entire cosmos. Everything is related to everything, and that is especially true of nature. An oil spill off the coast of Alaska has far-reaching effects on water, on shore life, and on eco-systems, including plants, animals, and humans.

The creation story found in the book of Genesis relates a command to the first earthlings to "subdue the earth." Tragically, "subdue" often has been interpreted as a license to violate, exploit, plunder, waste, and abuse.

stewardship v. dominion

It is a misreading of the text to think that human beings can do whatever they want to the Earth because God gave them permission and power. As human beings we do have a unique power in our relationship to the Earth, but that power must become a partnership of reverence and preservation.

Obviously, there is a need for new metaphors and better theological thinking as we move into the next century. Nature, in all its wildness and beauty, can be a spiritual touchstone, but only if it is sustained and allowed to generate new life again and again. For me, one positive way of thinking about nature comes from process philosophers and theologians. For those not familiar with process thinking, it has its roots in the work of Alfred North Whitehead, who was first a mathematician and only later a philosopher. Whitehead understood the "radical internal connections" of all reality. That is to say, every past moment of reality pours into a present moment, and then that present moment moves into the future, only to become past, then present, then future, then past, then present over and over again as all reality exists in a process of becoming. This means that all things are deeply connected and relational. It's not that I begin to think of the world relationally; the world is in its most essential being relationally connected. Process thinking offers a more organic view of reality, a world in which all things are connected and in which there flows a life energy that animates each and every moment of existence.

The implications of Whitehead's understanding of reality have been taken up by many theologians who appreciate the interrelatedness of Whitehead's philosophy and who have wanted new metaphors for understanding God and nature. In her book *Models of God: Theology for an Ecological, Nuclear Age*, Sallie McFague offers an enchanting metaphor for God and the world. I'm not suggesting that McFague is a process theologian, only that she offers a metaphor certainly agreeable with process thinking. She suggests that we should think of the earth as the *body of God*.

I like this image for several reasons. First, hardly anything is more beautiful than the human body. Artists have known this for centuries. Second, the body is a holistic image. It's not enough to have an arm. Not enough to have a toe. Not enough to have an ear. The body functions only when there is a degree of interrelatedness and wholeness. Don't forget the old ditty: "The hip bone's connected to the leg bone; the leg bone's connected to the…" Third, the image of body is important because it requires ongoing nurturing. Hair must be combed. Teeth must be brushed. Toenails trimmed. Fourth, the body needs replenishment. In some ways, the body is always dying and then reproducing itself. It works on the cycle of putting in and then putting out. Yet, if there is no putting in of food and water, the body suffers, and eventually the glorious cycle of life is broken. Fifth, the body image is nice because the body both works and plays. As I mentioned earlier, both work and play can be sacred. The Earth also can bring playful joy—the New Mexico landscape outside Santa Fe. But the Earth also can work—solar power, a hydroelectric dam, soil producing food, rain providing water, and so on.

The French theologian Pierre Teilhard de Chardin wrote of a "communion with God through the earth." This is touchstone theology! If the earth is the body of God, God is deeply related to the world. When I touch the earth, I am touching God. This is why so many mystical, numinous, luminous moments happen to us in nature. To see the Grand Canyon is to see the splendor of the body of God. To see the mountains of Tibet is to see incredible dimensions of God. This is why there was so much silence in the car while we drove to Ghost Ranch. Yes, there was the occasional outburst of praise—"Awesome!" "Beautiful!" But more than words, deeper than words, there was silence—which, of course, is exactly the right response before God.

Surely we know this to be true in other places of our lives. For instance, when I reach out and touch my wife, knowing her body like a familiar map after nearly twenty years of marriage, I still experience the joyful essence of her being. It's more than physical pleasure. It's more than simple biological fulfillment. I come close to her deepest sense of soul. In the same way, when we touch the earth it is like touching the soul of God. The mountains, the oceans, the rivers, all become the body of God.

And if this is so, it is important for our spiritual quest that we find ways of touching the sacred rhythms of earth and sky. A garden. A hike. A walk along the beach. Seeing, really seeing, a sunset. And if this is so, this earth as the body of God, we must find ways of reducing consumption so the earth can survive. And if this is so, we must find ways to put back into the earth while we reduce what we take from the earth. And if this is so, every positive ecological step we take ultimately is our way of caring for God. And if this is so, this mystery of God and earth, we must walk with reverence upon this earth because all of life is, as Gerard Manley Hopkins wrote, "charged with the glory of God."

In his book *The Gift: Imagination and the Erotic Life of Property*, Lewis Hyde paints a vivid scene depicting two distinct human viewpoints toward nature. He notes that when the Puritans landed in Massachusetts, they quickly noticed a peculiar quality to how Native Americans understood property and possessions. For the white Europeans, to receive a gift from the Native Americans meant they then owned and possessed the gift. Who knows, maybe they planned on shipping the gift back to the British Museum or turning the gift into an artifact. This, however, was not the viewpoint of the Native Americans. When they gave a gift, they just assumed that the gift would be passed back to them so that they might then be able to pass the gift on to others. This is where the derogatory term "Indian giver" emerged. Crucial to the Native American viewpoint of possessions was the idea of movement, activity, and temporary custody of any particular item. No one really "owns" anything, especially nature and property. How could one really own ocean or sky or mountain? Rather than seeing nature as something to possess, the Native American tradition emphasized the sacred responsibility of caring for nature and keeping it flowing.

Could it be the case that one way of understanding nature is to see that it is indeed a touchstone for our spiritual aliveness and, furthermore, that we have only a brief time to care for it, nurture it, love it, even as we would love the body of a spouse or child? Could it be that the sacredness of nature is due, in part, to nature's being God's body and that, like all bodies we grow to love, including our own, we have limited opportunities to experience it and, therefore, should never squander the spiritual possibilities of experiencing nature? And could it be that our relationship to the earth is so radically temporary that we should have as our ultimate goal both how treatment of the earth will make God feel and how our treatment of the earth will be received by the next generation? These are questions that start in the world of feeling, but must conclude in the world of attitudes and actions.

Jung's Green Christ

I find it fascinating that the great psychologist Carl Gustav Jung had a dream that vividly brought together the religious and earthly elements of life. By way of background, it is helpful to remember that Jung was the son of a clergyman and was reared in a family deeply influenced by traditional Christian symbols. In his book *Memories, Dreams, and Reflections,* Jung recounts a dream that gives some insight into his upbringing in this highly religious environment. But more than a representation of Jung's personal psychology, this dream gives insight into a major shift in twentieth-century reality.

In this dream, Jung sees a great cathedral. The cathedral is an obvious container for Christian energy and holy presence. In the cathedral God speaks, is experienced, and in the cathedral people gather to be in the presence of the Divine. In Jung's dream, a young boy sees the beautiful cathedral. It is gleaming. Above the cathedral, he sees the throne of God. This is consistent with the idea that the cathedral is the *axis mundi,* the center of the earth. All is right with the world when the cathedral is in its place and God is present. Then, carrying with it all the repulsion and disgust that one might imagine, God defecates upon the cathedral, smashing the ceiling, the walls, completely destroying the beautiful building.

The significance of this dream is far-reaching. But rather than using it as a road map into Jung's psyche, I would suggest that we follow the insight of Jungian scholar Murray Stein, who understands the dream as an indication of a major cultural shift—namely, that no one religious tradition, no one religious container can hold the presence of God's holy energy in the world. Not long ago the *New York Times* devoted an entire Sunday magazine to the topic "The Decentralization of God." And that is surely happening in our society. Every religion is in and of itself complete, but it is not the only complete system of religious consciousness in the world.

Jung understood the destruction of the cathedral as an indication that what people really need is an immediate, living experience of the presence of God. Not mediated through the church. Not held in the container of the cathedral or temple or ashram alone. And certainly not a bibliolatry found in so many fundamentalist churches, the thinking that the Bible alone contains all religious truth. What is needed is a charged divinity that fills all places, is available to all people, an energy that is defined as tremendous mystery.

With that as background, I want to relate one more dream of Professor Jung's. This one came to him as a vision. In it he sees a dramatic presentation of light at the foot of his bed. And in the light he makes out the figure. It is Christ on the cross. Jung recalls that it was marvelous and beautiful. But what is so significant about the dream is that the Christ figure had a body made of greenish gold. For Jung, the alchemical significance of the greenish gold was life-changing.

The color green is symbolic of nature. Lush. Living. Verdant. To experience green is to experience the organic aliveness of nature. The green Christ is the nature Christ or the Christ found in nature. The gold color in Jung's dream reflects that metallic quality of life, mineral and stone, but God is found even there. Jung would write of this dream that it clearly showed him the union of spirit and matter.

Jung's dream of the green Christ helps me remember a dream I had more than a decade ago. In this dream I am standing in the pulpit preaching a sermon. Then suddenly, as if moved by the presence of God, I start skipping up the center aisle of my church crying out joyfully, "Let the Spirit in! Let the Spirit in! Let the Spirit in!" But while running up the aisle, I notice that there are pieces of green jade set in the tile. Beautiful green jade. This green so catches my eye that I can still remember it with amazing precision. What is helpful to me is that, unlike Jung's cathedral that is destroyed by God, I experienced the feeling mode of green within the house of God! The green Christ and the green jade point to the "green" reality of God in the world, and that is why nature is such an important spiritual touchstone.

I often have chided my clergy friends—a favorite pastime of mine, by the way—that one of these days they should stop taking all those trips to Israel and the "Holy Land" and go to the real holy land—Big Sur, California, or the Sangre de Christo Mountains of New Mexico. That's real holy land! I'm kidding them, of course, but only halfway. These places have become for me holy ground and holy land. In these landscapes of nature, their textures and odors and sights, I have touched the green Christ and have been brought back to life again and again. And even when I am not there, the memory of these places lingers inside me. Sometimes, closing my eyes, I am almost there—almost, because "there" is "here," here in the deepest home of my soul. And I am sure you can recount your places of holy ground, moments when in the presence of rock or mountain or water you felt yourself strangely and wonderfully at home. Nature is a sacred touchstone, a sacrament every bit as powerful as bread and wine.

Touching the Wild and Gentle

One dimension of nature that has the power to become a spiritual touchstone is the human interaction with animals. Whether in real life or through images in film and books, animals carry a wild and gentle spirit that touches and transforms life. They represent dimensions of who we are or who we aspire to be. They carry psychological energy, a certain spiritual weight. Being in the presence of animals can create new self-understanding or spiritual calm or even the experience of unconditional love. In this sense, animals function for people the way people have traditionally understood the functioning of angels. They bring healing, help, hope to our lives, moving us to experience life more deeply and more meaningfully. It should come as no surprise that "pet therapy" is gaining in popularity as a way of ministering to the human spirit.

Several years ago, I took my son Matthew, who was ten years old at the time, to the zoo in Indianapolis. At that time it was a new zoo, one of the best in the country. There was a great deal of excitement over the opening of the zoo's new whale and dolphin pavilion. We were there on a June afternoon. Walking down the steps into the pavilion, we found darkness and the musty feel of moisture. In the pavilion itself, we looked through large panes of glass into an enormous aquarium. Dolphins were swimming in it.

There is something mystical about dolphins. They move with such grace, such ease through the water. They possess a language of communication that they use among themselves, but they also seem to be on the verge of communicating with human beings. And then there is that perpetual smile, personifying a kind of joy that often seems elusive to the human experience. To see a dolphin swim is to witness flowing animal poetry.

Maybe it's because they swim in the ocean, that symbolic place of the unconscious, that dolphins have such an intriguing connection to humans. Maybe it is that as human beings we were designed to live in the unconscious—that deepest place of our being—but we moved to land prematurely or have stayed on land too long, that we need to dive again into the oceanic depths of our own soul. Maybe the dolphin symbolizes some playfulness that has been lost in the human experience. We all came from water, the primordial waters of creation, but also the embryonic waters inside our mothers, and perhaps when we see a dolphin we are seeing a call to reconnect with our originality. Is it the case that to see a dolphin at home in the water is to glimpse what is possible inside the home of our own soul? I can't fully explain it, but when I see a dolphin, something in my soul is stirred, is inspired, is deeply engaged.

Matthew and I were in the pavilion at the zoo watching the dolphins. There were six, if I remember correctly, and both of us were mesmerized by their effortless swimming and playful existence. Suddenly, something unforgettable happened. Matthew reached out his arm and, with his right index finger completely extended, pointed toward one particular dolphin, touching the glass with the tip of his finger. Then this dolphin, though it was nearly on the other side of the huge tank, began to swim toward the glass. Slowly it moved closer, closer, closer until it came to the place where Matthew was standing. And when it arrived, it suspended itself in deft stillness, and touched its nose right at the place where Matthew's finger was touching the glass. Both Matthew and the dolphin were in perfect stillness with one another, frozen for several seconds, and then the dolphin swam away.

It was a moment of such grace, such beauty, that it is difficult to describe completely the full mystical quality of it. Something wild and gentle had come close to him. It was numinous. Mystical. Transcendent, yet earthly at the same time. And his response, interestingly enough, was not, "Wow, Dad, wasn't that neat!" Instead, he was silent. I remember that we walked away in silence, and he didn't say a word for the longest time. I knew better than to bring it up myself. There was something so awesome, so beautiful about that encounter with the dolphin that it was beyond words. The dolphin connected with Matthew, and Matthew connected with the dolphin in a way that is hard to explain, except to say that it was for Matthew a touchstone moment.

Since that time, Matthew has had other experiences with animals. He's been to Africa and has seen giraffes and elephants. He's helped take care of a family pet, our dog, Lucy. He's been on whale-watching boats and witnessed the great tail fin break through to the sky and then slap the water with an explosion of white water. He had another experience once, sitting on a rocky beach at Point Lobos Nature Reserve in California, when a seal crawled up to him on the rocks, rested a foot away for nearly an hour, and then slid back into the sea. How could such a thing happen? It can't be predicted or planned. Something in the animals and in him are drawn together. These animal experiences, along with his dolphin moment, continue to define his life.

What I find is that most people either have a favorite landscape or a favorite animal story that has become for them spiritually defining. This is so because nature and animals and the experience of the natural world embody for us the divine presence. After the publication of my first book, *Finding a Faith That Makes Sense*, I was surprised at the response elicited by a brief sentence in my acknowledgments. There I mentioned my black Labrador, Lucy, who had become for me "an angel while writing the book." It remains so even today as I am writing. I sit at a table, and she is on the sofa, half awake, watching, waiting patiently for me to take her for a run on the beach. But the reaction to the mere mention of my "dog angel" drew so many responses from readers that it cannot be overlooked. "I have an angel too," said one woman. Still another told me, "After my divorce, I don't think I would have made it without my two cats. They were my angels…" One friend actually sent me a Christmas ornament, a black Labrador dressed in a white flowing robe of an angel. There is a mystical bond people experience between themselves and animals; they become touchstones for our spiritual aliveness.

That the significance of animals in our lives cannot be underestimated I know from personal experience. Just a few days ago, close to ten years after Matthew and I made that trip to the Indianapolis Zoo, I asked him, "Matt, do you remember that time at the zoo in Indianapolis when we went to the whale and dolphin pavilion? Do you remember anything special that happened that day?"

He said, "Yeah, I remember. I was standing right up to the glass, and a dolphin came right over to me and stayed there a long time."

I said, "Oh, so you do remember. What did that feel like?"

He smiled. It was the same smile he had when he was ten years old. I miss that smile sometimes. This young man, this child, smiled and said, "I felt like I made a friend."

That's a living touchstone, something wild and gentle, that forever will be with my son. These animals we touch or see or care for, these animals make us human beings fully alive. That's why they are so important to our lives. That dolphin always will be inside my son. And also always inside his father.

Finding Real Humility

I used to think of humility as an attitude of meekness, quietness, verging on passivity. But true humility is quite different from this stereotypical definition. Humility, related to the word *humus*, means being deeply and radically connected to the earth. To walk humbly with God or to live with an attitude of humility means that we are connected to the earth in all its complexity and beauty. To be humble is to be earthy.

In the biblical story of creation, the first human beings could be understood and even translated as *earthlings*. An earthling is someone who is intimately connected to the earth. Presently, our culture seems to be fascinated with space aliens. Entire religious cults are being propagated around the idea that we can transcend earthly life and find our ultimate destiny in spaceships, stars, and other planets. In 1996, the top-grossing movie was *Independence Day*, a movie about a space invasion from another planet. I don't mind such flights of imagination, but at some point as human beings we must discover the beauty and fullness of earthly existence. This is humility. To be humble means that we appreciate the sacred and mysterious earth connections present in our bodies. No wonder the Genesis creation story portrays man and woman as being created from dust and bone. This is real humility.

Wendell Berry once offered the insight in an essay that when a man would buy a farm in Kentucky, he would eventually "get off his horse and walk the land." There is much that stops us in contemporary life from "getting off our horses." We drive in speeding automobiles, normally on interstate highways that have flattened out the texture of American landscape. We cocoon in houses protected from the environment. If we go on vacation, it is often focused on amusement. Think about it—no matter how well it is marketed, Disney World is still not real! The only thing real in Florida are the swamps and Everglades, and even they are now strained because of human encroachment.

Part of our spiritual life is rediscovering our earthling existence. To be humble is to get dusty, or at least to get in touch with the dustiness of our humanity. This is what Berry meant when he suggested we needed to get off our horses. Feeling a landscape, any landscape, is such an important step in spiritual consciousness. I certainly don't want to leave the impression that one must find a wilderness area such as the high desert of New Mexico to find this awareness. There are mini-landscapes to be appreciated. If you live in New York City, there are the parks. If you live in Charleston, South Carolina, there are the hidden courtyards. If you are in Chicago, there is the Lake Michigan shoreline. If you live in a high-rise apartment building, there are the house plants and herbs that can be nurtured like old friends. If you live in Los Angeles, there is that quiet morning hour before you have to merge on the freeway, a time of feeling the coolness of ocean air. Not everyone can go to the holy land of Big Sur or New Mexico, but everyone can accent his or her earthly connections by cultivating humility.

Francis Ponge once wrote of poetry, saying, "[Poetry] is to nourish the spirit of man by giving him the cosmos to suckle. We have only to lower our standard of dominating nature and to raise our standard of participating in it in order to make the reconciliation take place."[4] I like what Ponge has said, especially the image of finding a cosmos to suckle. This is true humility, and it is also the beginning of the knowledge of God. To be humble is to nurse the cosmos, caring for it and nurturing it, and—to follow Sallie McFague's image—we also are nursed by the cosmos, taking in the milk of landscape and nature. This is why so many people I know find that their most religious moments have been moments in nature. The cosmos is taking us to her breast and giving us milk. It is in the wonder of receiving and giving life that we find the essence of true humility and, in turn, true humanity.

Feminine Energy and Mother Nature

As a child I remember a television commercial for a particular margarine, the gist of it being that this particular margarine tasted as good as butter. The clinching line, however, was spoken by a woman who was dressed up like Mother Nature. After being fooled by the butter-like taste of the margarine, she created an angry display of lightning and then said, "It's not nice to fool Mother Nature!"

For most of us, Mother Nature is little more than a turn-of-phrase, a casual expression usually connected to the weather. If there is a flood, we might say, "Mother Nature sure was harsh today." Or a destructive storm might be summarized by saying, "Mother Nature unleashed her fury last night." And if not a casual remark, the idea of Mother Nature is that of a character in an antiquated view of reality. The stuff of fairy tales and myths. Understanding the world from a scientific viewpoint has all but eliminated any concept of Mother Nature.

I too want to dismiss this casual idea of Mother Nature. I do not believe, for example, that an angry woman is behind every thunderstorm or earthquake. Nor do I think she cares about the difference between butter and margarine! To literalize Mother Nature in this way is to miss the real significance of her place in myth and religion. What is behind the concept of Mother Nature? That is the question I find most helpful. I would affirm with great joy the reality underneath the symbol of Mother Nature because she symbolizes the feminine life force that exists in the universe. This is the life force of birthing, growing, nurturing. The feminine life force is bodily. Shaped by natural rhythms and cycles. There is something dark and bloody and moist about this feminine energy. Even women themselves talk about the ticking of their biological clocks. Seeing the ocean, wave after wave after wave, is to be in the presence of feminine energy. Traditionally, the sun has been understood as masculine and the moon a symbol of the feminine. Mother Nature is moon energy released into the world.

Having a teenage daughter, I now see her growing and becoming part of a natural, bodily, feminine cycle of life. I also see how my wife beautifully celebrates each of our daughter's bodily changes, explaining and giving indispensable facts. But along with the facts, she celebrates with Katie the mystery of her growing feminine powers.

To say that there is a Mother Nature is another way of saying that the divine being in the universe has feminine dimensions. God is not a physical woman any more than God is a physical man. But to learn to pray to the Mother God of the universe, as well as imaging the Divine as a Father God, is a way of acknowledging the deep presence of the feminine within the natural world. I find it fascinating that in the Roman Catholic Church the presence of the Virgin Mary is related to the divine feminine. My suspicion is that Mary actually completes the divine being, moving from a male-dominated trinity to a quaternity of Father (male), Son (male), Holy Spirit (feminine), and Mary (feminine). I'm not dogmatic about that, but it makes some sense to me. Regardless, the intuition to look at the natural world and call it Mother Nature is a good intuition and perfectly in tune with what is real. From my perspective, the divine being is in all things—panentheism—and in the working of all things there is birth, growth, nurture, death, birth, growth, nurture, death, and so it goes in an endless cycle of life. This is the feminine quality of the Divine expressed in the bodily places of the natural world.

And if this is true, the way we access the divine feminine in nature is to open our own bodily senses to welcome her into our own experiences. We can't simply think our way into the places of Mother Nature. Mother Nature works through our senses. She must be experienced more than studied, invited more than pursued. As I have tried to say elsewhere, to be sensual is not the same as being sexual. Sexuality should be sensual if it is truly to be a mutually enlivening experience, but sensuality is much broader. To be sensual is to open the door for the divine feminine to touch our lives.

There are a variety of ways to cultivate a more sensual lifestyle with nature. Sensuality means awakening to textures. The feel of a blade of grass and the feel of a leaf are two different experiences. Sensuality appreciates the distinctiveness of touch. Moving away from a Teflon world where everything is indistinguishable and slick, sensuality appreciates the many textures of human experience.

Sensuality means awakening to smells. Aromatherapy contends that in certain smells our body finds healing and wholeness. It is true. The smells of New Mexico are not the same as those of Texas, and in the morning, when I smelled piñon wood burning in the fireplace of my hotel lobby in Santa Fe, it became for me a life-giving aroma! It's a smell that's out of this world. No, deeply in this world! Smelling the world is wonderful.

Sensuality means awakening to sights. To see—really, deeply, joyfully see—is one of life's great pleasures. The spectrum of light provides vividness to our lives. Not just color, but shading and shadowing, seeing the ordinary as if it were extraordinary. That's the sensuality of seeing.

Sensuality means awakening to sounds. Far too often we go through days, even weeks, and never appreciate sounds. The sound of a bird. The sound of leaves rustling. The sound of water running. The sound even of pots clanging and glasses clinking in the kitchen. There is a poetry to sounds. Much of poetry is the artistic juxtaposition of sound.

Sensuality means awakening to tastes. If it's the case that Mother Nature gives us our food, the peaches and apples and tomatoes that touch our palette, then we experience the Divine by genuinely tasting the gifts of her work. To taste is to love God!

Looking back on my day at Ghost Ranch in New Mexico, I realize that it was more than merely being in a beautiful place. It was beautiful to be sure. But more than the rugged beauty, I experienced an aliveness of spiritual quality that I will not soon forget. In the texture of landscape, the sight of color, the smell of plants and animals, even in the feel of dust under my feet, I came close to my own dust, animated by the generative spirit of God, a green feminine energy that brought me to life. This is the power of nature. To stand in it. Be touched by it. To be in the great cathedral of the world.

Chapter 8

Community: Building the Human Family

In the city of San Francisco, there is a man on the corner of Mission Street, sitting on the sidewalk. He is disheveled. Unshaven. His head droops as if he is in some kind of stupor. A large garbage bag next to him is filled with a few cans, a ratty-looking blanket, a pair of tennis shoes, and some fruit that looks to be on the verge of rotting.

Who is this man? What is his story? What happened to his life? And more important, what is your relationship to him? Do you walk on the other side of the street? Do you avoid him? Does he look dangerous to you? Threatening? Menacing? Do you have any eye contact with him as you walk past?

Right now a young mother in Honduras is holding her baby. The baby is dying. Simple medicine, so readily available in the United States or Europe, could bring this baby back to life. But there will be no medicine. The mother will walk to a village, and there she will sit exhausted in a small hut. She will look for some food. Some comfort. Maybe a missionary nurse. But in a few days this baby will die.

How do you feel about that mother? Does she say anything to you? Do you feel anything toward her? To you and me the child is nameless, but not to this mother. As far as most of the human race is concerned, this mother is nameless too. You can live your entire life and never think of them again. But they are living human beings, aren't they? Each possesses some human significance and value. They both have dark, beautiful eyes, lovely skin, and each of them has known feelings of gentle comfort and sweet love. Who is this woman, this baby?

Sitting across the table from me is a man. We are approximately the same age. He is bright, confident. He tells me of loving art and music. We talk about favorite restaurants. The best cafes in town. We both like a good cappuccino or latte. This is the first time we have met, but surprisingly he takes the conversation deeper. He tells me of his childhood. Yes, a church background. Very conservative. He tells me of loving and supportive parents. He tells me of going to college and coming to terms with a long, agonizing awareness that something inside, to put it in his own words, "something inside his soul was different." He tells me about the time he first told his mother and father that he was gay. Not easy. The hardest conversation he ever had in his life. "Things were never the same," he said. "They tried to understand," he said, "but things were never the same."

And then he told me of his struggle with church and faith and community. He told me of cruel hatred and less than polite avoidance by old friends. He told me of heartache and hope. He said it right to my face, "You cannot understand what it's like to be a gay man here in this city." And the way he said it, the way he punctuated his beginning "you," the way the words "cannot understand" clipped off his tongue with acid sureness, I knew he was speaking human truth to me.

Do I need this man? Does this man need me? We are so different. Or are we? It certainly would appear so. I am married. Three children. What in the world might bring us together? And what about you? Do you need this man? Is he somehow in your psyche too? He also wants to know if he might find a place in the church that I love and serve. "Would they welcome me?" he asked. Sometimes churches don't accept people the way they need to be accepted. That doesn't say enough. Sometimes churches can be cruel and exclusive. How would you answer that question? Would you, could you, offer the gift of acceptance?

A woman is working in a large corporation. It could be IBM. Southwestern Bell. Microsoft. She has been with the company for years. She notices that promotions seems to fly over her head like a speeding airplane. Nothing seems to land on her career runway. She observes that the guys in the office go out to lunch with each other. She's never invited. Maybe when there's a formal meeting, but never on an informal basis. She finds herself wondering, "What do they talk about at lunch? Don't they like me? Are they afraid of me? Have I done something wrong?"

When they are entertaining clients, they rarely ask her to go see the basketball game at night. Maybe they assume she wouldn't be interested in the basketball game. Maybe they think she would rather be home with her family. Maybe someone is making decisions about her without consulting her. Has she become invisible? Do people look right through her because she is a woman? The sexual leering stopped years ago. They have too much respect for her to do that. But something else is happening, something more subtle, more pernicious; she is being excluded quietly from the possibilities of the work community.

Do you know this woman? Have you seen her, thought about her? Is she your wife? Your mother? Your daughter? Are you this woman? And even more to the point, are you and I to some degree responsible for her marginalization? Is she invisible to us because we have failed to see women as fully capable, fully intellectual, fully creative partners in the human experience of work and productivity? Not harassment exactly, but a lack of appreciation for the gift of partnership that might exist if we could see her differently. Do you need for this woman to find a better place in the world? Does it matter to you? Does it affect you?

Human community is wondrous, beautiful, and strong. Human community is fragile, tentative, and vulnerable. Do we need human community? Can it touch us, enrich our lives, make us whole? Can human community be a touchstone for our growth as people? Is there something in us that will never develop fully until we learn to touch a global family? Can a way of thinking and perceiving the world actually make a difference in the world, even within our own souls? These are the questions I wrestle with as I think about the touchstone of human community.

Unlike relationships addressed earlier in this book, community is a broader concept. Relationships demand that we be in close proximity, intimately connected, and even that a degree of personal commitment must be present. But community is different. In community we are related to one another, not because we know one another, but because we share a common humanity. Community is the neighbor across the street, but community is also the neighbor across the sea. Community is the plight and future being carved out, not only by our own children, but by all children of the world. To live in community is to live in awareness that the world is small, that the human family is one, that the destiny of one becomes the destiny of all.

Community takes so many different forms. Community can be an attitude. For example, making the decision to overturn affirmative action says a lot about our view of community. Providing tax breaks only for the wealthy says a lot about community. Treating elderly persons as if they have nothing to offer our society is a particular posture toward community. Believing that one race or one gender or one culture is intrinsically superior to all others is a kind of stance toward community. On the other hand, when people live with heightened sensitivity toward children, with such attitudes as can be found in organizations such as the Children's Defense Fund, that is an attitude toward community that becomes life-giving. The hospice program embodies a positive attitude toward community, especially for those in the tender moment of dying. Members of Rotary clubs or Kiwanis clubs, people who give so much back to people, have a certain understanding of community. Community, therefore, is embedded deep within our broadly conceived attitudes about others.

Community also is expressed in organizational life. It may seem strange to think of organizations as intimately related to the spiritual life. For many, organizations—particularly organized religion—have been a detriment to the spiritual life. As one friend recently said, "I quit going to church because no one was helping me discover my spiritual calling." Sadly, this is true of many churches. But not all churches. Organizations have the power to embody hopes and aspirations that bring healing to community. I think all religions are able to do this. At its best, organized religion found in churches and synagogues and temples can touch the soul with inspiration and ground the soul in the reality of community. Spiritual wholeness is not just about soaring into the sky with beautiful insight; sometimes spiritual aliveness is learning how to serve soup at a homeless shelter. The challenge, of course, is for organizations to ground us positively in the concerns of community without grinding us into a sterile bureaucracy of organization.

The Household of God

Within the Christian faith is a concept called ecumenism. Ecumenism—or the ecumenical movement, as it is sometimes called—is named after a Greek word, *oikoumene*. I touched on this concept earlier in the book. *Oikoumene* literally means *"the household."* The Christian faith takes this concept of the household and connects it to God. The ecumenical movement is about the household of God, the global unity of all Christians.

In his farewell address to his friends, Jesus prays that his disciples "may...be one" (John 17:21a). This prayer for unity goes to the heart of the Christian gospel, namely, that all people might experience unity with God and with one another. Sin, rather than being understood as the breaking of some arbitrary rule, is actually the fracturing of relationship that happens within the wondrous web of creation.

This idea of a household of God offers a variety of helpful insights. It first of all suggests that at the heart of the world is the divine presence of God. The theologian Paul Tillich understood God as the "ground of all being." That was Tillich's way of suggesting that divine reality is pervasive, at once transcendent and immanent. To think of God as some anthropomorphic being "up there" finally does not capture the all-encompassing reality of divinity. The world is the household of God. This means that God is near to all. Not to some, but to all. Not to some select people, but to all. Not to some particular culture, but to all.

This is especially important to appreciate given the human tendency to identify God with a particular religion or nation or ideology. There is nothing wrong with religious conviction. I encourage people each week in my congregation to rediscover passion in their faith. But religious passion that becomes exclusive or arrogant or over against all other religious expression becomes dangerous and, in the end, damages the very community religion should be seeking to heal. Almost every world religion has some form of religious fundamentalism, and the problem with fundamentalism is that it tends to breed intolerance and violence toward others. Sometimes that violence has been literal—the crusades of the Middle Ages, for example, or the Jewish Holocaust, to name another unforgettable moment of the breakdown of the household of God. To list the number of times religious zeal has done violence to fellow human beings would be fruitless and exhausting. Yet, at its best, religious faith reminds people of their interrelationship to all other people.

The household image suggests that all people finally are held together by a depth of unity that cannot or should not ever be ignored. People need not invent oneness for the human family; oneness with others is at the heart of what it means to be human. To be ecumenical in spirit means to awaken to the reality of human oneness that already is present in the world. All that breaks community—racism, ageism, sexism, nationalism—is tragic because it betrays the fundamental oneness of humanity.

For Christians, this idea of ecumenism has had two distinct stages. One stage has been to recognize the oneness of all Christians. This is no small insight, and I would never want to underestimate it. For years, the American religious landscape was characterized by Presbyterians who thought they were superior to Methodists and Methodists who thought they were superior to Baptists and Baptists who thought they were superior to Roman Catholics. This unfortunate disunity often defined the Christian faith in terms of exclusivity, hostility, and, in some cases, hatred. This climate of distrust and competition was unfortunate and unnecessary.

Because of an emphasis on ecumenism in the twentieth century, most Christians now appreciate that although they may come from different denominations, an essential unity transcends denominational lines. This is a spiritual unity in Christ, a unity that reminds Christians that more unites us than divides us. The inadequacy, however, of Christian ecumenism is that there has not been enough emphasis on an ecumenical vision that embraces all people of all faiths and cultures. Isn't there a unity between Christian and Jew? Isn't there a unity between Jew and Buddhist? Isn't there a unity between Hindu and Christian?

One image that is helpful to me is that of a mountain. Mountains forever have been symbols of the divine journey. To climb the mountain is to seek God. As a Christian, I am climbing a mountain. My way of seeking God is marked particularly by the life of Jesus. On his journey, Jesus discovered and, in fact, left for me in the tradition of the church many markers that help me as I climb this enormous mountain of God. As I journey, it is so easy for me to assume that the path I am on is the only path. Why would I think there would be other paths? I see only the path I am on. Climbing my particular path takes all the energy and focus I can muster. Yet, at this place in the spiritual evolution of people, I now realize that this mountain is so large, so expansive, that there are others climbing the mountain too. In fact, if I could somehow take an aerial view of the mountain, I would see that there are indeed Christians climbing the mountain of God. To my surprise, other mountain expeditions are going on too. Other people of faith. Other markers on the paths. The other people who are climbing are just as sincere as, maybe more than, the people who are climbing with me on my path. If I take time to notice their path closely, I might even learn how to walk my path better. I don't have to walk their path—that is, I don't have to become Jewish or Buddhist or Islamic. But how enriching it would be if I could appreciate and learn from the path they are walking. A oneness exists among all people who climb—whether running or walking or crawling—upon the mountain of God. This kind of appreciation for the household of God becomes a touchstone of spiritual aliveness.

Today I am writing this chapter on an airplane. I am sitting in row four. Several things are happening at this very moment. I am sitting in the row of seats immediately behind first class. I am watching the people in first class receive their drinks. They are eating their meals. The flight attendant is giving them impeccable attention. I too have received a meal, though more modest than theirs. I have a flight attendant as well, but she is unable to give me the same level of attention as the passengers in first class are receiving. Sitting next to me is a young man from Korea. He looks to be in his early thirties. He doesn't speak much English. I helped him find a place for a large package before we left the airport in Denver. Now the captain has announced that we are going to fly through some turbulence and that we should fasten our seat belts until further notice. The ride is starting to get a bit rough. I don't really care to fly, but I feel especially anxious in this turbulence.

Because I have a vivid literary imagination combined with a lifelong anxiety about flying, I begin to wonder about the possibility of a tragic accident. That's what I'm worrying about right now. In a plane accident it doesn't matter if you are in first class or business class or coach class. It doesn't matter that some meals are better than others. It doesn't matter if I am an American and the person sitting next to me is Korean. It doesn't matter that I have a doctorate or that the person sitting behind me is only a high school graduate. It doesn't matter that the person in front of me has a net worth ten times that of my own. What matters on a plane is that all the travelers arrive safely, because unless we all arrive together, we will not arrive at all.

The *oikoumene* of God recognizes that there is essentially and beautifully one human community. That we are all fellow travelers climbing the same mountain of God is not just a statement of reality; it is a perspective with which to live. My stance cannot be isolationist, "I am a rock, I am an island." My stance cannot be one of arrogance, "God loves *me*. God loves *us*." My stance cannot even be one of benign tolerance, "Live and let live." Instead, if we are to become fully alive, a wondrous development of interconnections with people is called for—learning from one another, playing and working with one another, even loving one another.

Cornell West, in his brilliant book *Race Matters*, comes to the conclusion that if we are to heal the wounds and systemic proliferation of racism, two insights must be appreciated. One is that all citizens are fellow citizens. It's not just "them." It's never just "those." The "thems" and "thoses" are finally us; this is the human household. The other insight is remarkable. After all the programs, plans, and strategies for dealing with racism, West concludes that what is needed is love. Programs and policies are important, but until human beings can awaken to the potential and demand of love, the household of God will be forever fragmented.

Ecumenism reminds people of divine closeness and human unity. Additionally, the ecumenical emphasis awakens appreciation for diversity and pluralism. This can be illustrated in many ways. When I was a youngster, my mother prepared our dinners each night. She was a fine cook but not a particularly imaginative cook. Meat loaf. Mashed potatoes. Canned peas. A tuna casserole every now and then. For my early years, and I'm sure for a lot of others born and bred in the American heartland, that was my definition of food.

But as I grew up, left home, went off to college, off to live in or visit cities around the world, my world became bigger and more diverse. I have learned to love the intense sweetness of sun-dried tomatoes. As a child, I never tasted a sun-dried tomato, but now I can't imagine certain dishes without them. I don't remember ever eating fresh salmon as a child. Today, one of my favorite meals is to cook salmon on the grill, add a few wood chips for a nice smoked flavor, with maybe a little mango salsa on the side. By the way, I never ate a mango in my first eighteen years of growing up. I also have enjoyed Chinese food—Kung Pao chicken is my favorite. I like the Japanese cuisine of sushi. I love a good French pâté and a little wine. And now, living in Texas, ancho chilies have become a staple, along with pico de gallo, pinto beans, and rice. This diversity has brought a tremendous amount of delight and satisfaction to my life.

Diversity, though at times it might feel threatening, ultimately brings an intensity of experience that should not be missed. Coming from the household of God is a diversity of music and dance and poetry. Coming from the household of God is a diversity of ideas and concepts and perspectives. Coming from the household of God is a diversity of cuisine and culture and character. This diversity, rainbow-like and splashed with every color imaginable, makes life intense and fascinating. To flatten out the world into one texture or to paint the world with one color may at first provide a false sense of security. But in the end, it only makes life boring and meaningless. That's it exactly—diversity in the human family, no matter how it is expressed, brings more meaning, not less.

To live in community means that pluralism is to be celebrated. Faith will find many forms. Religion will be varied. Culture will overlap and diverge in fascinating ways. But in all the changes and challenges of community, people will be brought to life even as their awareness of interrelationship grows. The people who teach us this the most are those remarkable figures who seem to have a breathtaking viewpoint of the human experience. Jesus understood the essential oneness of humanity. And so did Gandhi. So did Martin Luther King, Jr. So did Mother Teresa. One world. One family. One journey.

The Call to Participate

If there is a household of humanity to which all people belong, surely that household must have organizational structures for its functioning and continued vitality. Participating in those structures is part of the touch-stone experience of life.

This area of the spiritual life, perhaps more than any other I have addressed in this book, creates anxiety and intense resistance. Walking along a beach and feeling the presence of God has a certain appeal for the spiritual seeker. And it should! But to suggest that belonging to an organization designed to help others, working on a long-term community project, attending monthly committee meetings that become tedious and difficult, or providing consistent and generous financial support for a charitable organization—suggestions such as these normally are resisted and disassociated from the quest for spiritual aliveness. Yet, if there is a household of God and if the well-being of all people is important and if it is true that the fate of one is reflective of the fate of all, I cannot ignore the fundamental call to participation.

A false division between the active life and the spiritual life must be rejected. The same must be said regarding the interior life and the exterior life. Outward journey touches inward journey; interior worlds of the soul transform the exterior worlds of the family of humanity. To participate in organizational life opens the door to self-understanding and creates an essential contribution to the larger network of life. Insofar as we ignore the call to participate in community, we impoverish our own sacred journey.

Typically, how one views community is shaped by larger cultural experiences, many of which we may not even be aware. For the generation of my parents and grandparents, participating in larger networks of public life was assumed. The government was experienced positively. Even when we went to war as a nation, such as happened in World War II, there was a strong consensus in society that as Americans we should support this cause. And citizens did support the cause. Some enlisted in the service, but many others stayed home and worked in community projects. There was a vital feeling of "being in this together." It's not the case that this generation loved war. They did not. It was more of a feeling that "whatever the greater needs of the nation, we will do our part to help satisfy them." After the war, citizens found ways to participate in society. A mother would attend a PTA meeting. A father might belong to the Kiwanis club or Rotary club. Most citizens would attend a church or synagogue weekly, working on countless committees and projects. And when election day appeared on the calendar, citizens would vote.

This participation in organizational life created a strong social fabric. Was there a downside to this participation? Looking back now, the answer obviously is yes. Love of country, for some, became a blind nationalism. The era of Joe McCarthy became ugly and violent, wrecking the lives of many. Some participated in larger networks of service, but never explored the depth of their own psychological being. No wonder Allan Ginsberg would write his infamous poem "Howl." In part, he was howling against a blind institutionalism. Therefore, on the one hand, there is something positive about this generational appreciation for organizational life, but on the other hand, there is something about it that needs critical correction.

Correction came with wild and furious intensity in the 1960s. The sterility of an earlier generation was called into question by another generation of Americans. Rather than seeing the value of organizational life, this generation saw all the flaws in the social fabric. This was the generation that I saw on the news each evening as a child. My first recollection of history is President Kennedy's funeral. The lone horse pulling the casket. Mrs. Kennedy veiled in black. The small children by her side. There was a loss of innocence for our nation that happened at that moment. And then there was the death of Martin Luther King, Jr. He was so powerful and so elegant and so authentic in his call for justice and peace. Soon after was the death of Robert Kennedy. Shot in a California hotel. It all played out over and over again as I watched his death on the television screen. All three of these men were involved in a larger vision for others. All public figures. All organizational leaders. All murdered.

And if that wasn't enough to disillusion us about participation in public life, there were the incessant protests against the Vietnam War. No longer were people saying, "Whatever the country does, we'll support it." Instead, there were vitriolic protests and speeches, many of them saying, "The government cannot be trusted." "The system is actually corrupt." "Don't trust anyone over forty." "Hell no, we won't go!" Rather than respecting and appreciating places of community authority, Americans saw these places as symbols of all that was wrong with the country. Storm the dean's office at the university. Burn the flag in front of the White House. Have a sit-in on the steps of the Capitol. Every place of authority became suspect, and community began to change radically.

During this time of tremendous social change, members of the National Guard were called in to check protesters at Kent State University. In a moment of madness and chaos, gunshots were fired. Students of that university were killed by the National Guard. How could anyone trust a government or organization that would do something like that? How could one work for a system, any system, with the potential to do this kind of human damage? About this time President Nixon, so paranoid about protecting his political power, authorized the Watergate break-in. In spite of all the good he had done—such as opening the door to China—

the president betrayed a fundamental agreement of trust with the American people. He blatantly lied about his undercover participation, but eventually he could not stop the unfolding truth of this political scheme. With perspiration pouring from his forehead, and his wife, Pat, stoically standing at his side, President Nixon resigned from office. Disgraced. Defeated. But more than that, a nation that at one time believed in common participation for the good of community was left reeling and retreating.

Since that time most Americans—although not all Americans—have had a less-than-enthusiastic relationship with organizational structures. There is suspicion of authority. There is doubt about organizational effectiveness. There is a pervasive individualism. A retreat from public life. I can't begin to tell you the number of times people have said to me, "I don't need the church to be a spiritual person." And it is true. One does not need organized religion to be religious. At the same time, a vitality is found in community life that simply cannot be experienced in isolation from others. Upon the broader landscape of public life, I suppose that a person can be a citizen in a democracy such as the United States and never vote or participate in community life, but the loss that this brings to the whole community and to our individual lives is incalculable. There is no democracy unless good people participate in it. There is no household of humanity unless responsible people in that family step up and care for it.

I think it is vital to the spiritual life of each person to hear and answer the call to service. It doesn't have to be heroic. It doesn't have to be all-encompassing. It doesn't have to save the entire world in one great swoop. It is the simple awareness that genuine community calls for genuine participation.

Jim Redwine is an amazing young man. He is not a "do gooder" in that naive sense of the phrase. He is a businessman. He has his hands full as a father of four children. Yet inside Jim is this realization that to be a part of a community one must give something back to a community. At a local elementary school in Fort Worth, Jim started volunteering his time. He talked to the principal and told her that he would like to spend Thursdays at the school just doing whatever needed to be done to help the staff and children. This was strictly volunteer work. No money. No glory. No recognition. Children and schools are important, and he wanted to make a contribution.

What has developed from this one answer of a call to service has been remarkable. The program has evolved to the point that a Thursday "Boys Club" now is thriving. After school, Jim has programming for these boys, playing ball, taking trips. But mostly it is an opportunity for these boys to have a safe environment in the presence of a caring and compassionate adult. Fun is the order of the day, but something deeper is happening. Lives are being shaped and transformed, all because one man heard the call to service and wanted to participate. What's fascinating to me is that Jim and I are nearly the same age. He saw the war protests on television. He saw one president shot, another resign, a civil rights leader murdered on the balcony of a Memphis hotel. These are the events that shaped his life too. Yet what could not be overcome inside him was this bright spark of participation in larger community life.

Hearing the call to service is like finding a candle inside our soul. Maybe it used to burn but has long since been extinguished. Maybe it has never been used. Maybe the candle is burning, but not brightly. The wick needs trimming and some excess wax must be poured off so that it can once again flame up and give light. No matter how good our relationships or how meaningful our rituals, no matter how much we enjoy nature or how delightful the telling of our personal stories, until we also connect and bring light to the larger stories of humanity, a part of us always will be in the dark. What Jim discovered was the grace of what Christians long ago called the commonweal, the common good for all citizens. To privatize our faith and spiritual journey is to miss the vitality that flows from the experience.

In Defense of Committees, Organizations, and Meetings

You may be thinking, "Meetings? Organizations? Committees? C'mon, I want to live the spiritual life. That's the problem with my life right now. Too busy! Too committed! I feel like I'm committeed and meetinged to death!"

Believe me, I understand and appreciate that sentiment. I'm the minister of a church of nearly 5,000 members. I know about committees. I sometimes think I could put a sign outside my door, "committees-r-us!" And as you can tell from the entire feeling in this book, I don't think the way to access spiritual aliveness is by becoming busier and busier. At the same time, I have found some sacred truths by participating in organizations. Organizations can become a sacrament, a conduit of grace. Participating in organizations can become a communion, a genuine moment of sharing. There is a wisdom I continue to find by virtue of the fact that I am willing to participate in organizational life. Maybe you'll find this wisdom to ring true inside your experience too.

Organizations teach me a great deal about human nature. Now that may seem strange given the fact that seeing human nature is such an obvious experience. But to see, really see, the humanity of others, is a marvel. On a committee working for a charity pancake breakfast or for the organizing of a community AIDS walk, even serving on a school board or city council, we see the humanity of others. Sometimes this humanity is inspiring. I'll never forget the church finance meeting when, to make the budget, every person on that committee raised his or her pledge 10 percent right there on the spot. No coercion. No pressure. Just plain and simple generosity toward a good cause. That kind of humanity is inspiring. I have seen our mayor in Fort Worth go into meetings where people were angry, bitter, and hostile. Yet because he was able to listen, genuinely listen, a transformation swept through the room, and by the end of the evening there was the beginning of consensus building. These are moments of beauty and grace found only in the mix of community.

I also have seen another side of humanity, not one that I necessarily want to see, but it is instructive and helpful nevertheless. I have seen anger in meetings. Political posturing in meetings. I have seen petty selfishness and ego display for self-importance. Yet this is humanity. The shadow side of human nature emerges in the context of organizations. Rather than being naive or even resistant to such realities, I find even those uncomfortable interactions have much to teach me about others and myself.

For one thing, if I find myself really resisting another person in an organization, it probably says a lot more about me than it does about that person. I'll never forget the time I demanded that one of my ministerial associates wear a suit and tie to work each day. I now realize that my reaction toward him was really my own anger for not having the courage to dress more casually myself. Yet without that interaction, I never would have had that insight. I find myself getting angry at people in committee meetings who are the most like me. Interesting, huh? In the interactions of community, I am able to learn and grow.

Sometimes when I see the shadow side of reality at work in organizations I am reminded that this is really how people are. We all, myself included, have our hurts and wounds. We all have our triggers of jealousy or anger or grief. To be naive to this complex side of people is to miss the beauty of the whole person. Recently I asked a friend who works in a high-tech, Silicon Valley company what it's like to work with his staff. He said, "Well, we play together at times, and we fight together at times, but that's what it is all about." To be naive and think that all people at all times are well intentioned is a great mistake. Community life requires that we see the complete picture of humanity, seeing others and ourselves.

Organizations also have the power to ground us in reality. It is important to dream. A house for abused children doesn't just happen in a city. Someone dreamed it. A scholarship fund doesn't just start. Someone first must feel it, see it, dream it. Dreams are wonderful because they bring us into a conversation with the future and what is possible. But life cannot be all dreams. At some point, dreams need to be grounded in reality. There is financial reality. The reality of personalities. The reality of a dream as it relates to other dreams and other realities. Organizations are needed because they give us critical awareness about what is both possible and relevant.

I may, for example, dream of starting a soup kitchen in my church for the homeless. That's a great dream. Who could argue with the goodness of that dream? But unless I check in with others, there's a good chance that the dream will never fly. In the larger organization, people will help me ask essential questions. "How will you fund the project? Who is going to work in the kitchen? Are you expecting us to do this? Where will we have the soup line? What about the fact that the kitchen already is being used by the preschool? How can we do both? Have you thought about working with another church? Does our community really need a soup kitchen? I thought one already existed. Is there another way, a better way we can help the homeless?"

Now the dreamer for the soup kitchen might hear these comments as resistance. And there might indeed be resistance in these questions. But do you see how these questions really ground the project? Every community project must go through three stages. The dream stage when it soars. The grounding stage when it is critically reviewed. And the launching stage when it takes off again with energy, strategy, and support. Without the vital link to community, the community is never served. Whether at work or in public government or volunteer organizations, engaging a network of people provides an essential grounding.

I need to add at this point that sometimes this grounding stage can be discouraging and maddening. Development of one of my dreams rarely happens as quickly as I want it to happen. Sometimes organizations can talk a project into the ground. It takes real skill to develop conversations that lead to action. Frequently, I want a one-year plan, and the committee wants a five-year plan. And frequently, I should hasten to confess, the dream needs five years! Sometimes in the grounding stage the dream becomes more than what I imagined. It's exciting when the creativity of community is unleashed. But what I know is that even the maddening pace of the organization has the power to teach me a great deal about myself and still get the project completed.

Another feature of organizations that is important to keep in mind is that they do, albeit at times slowly, get things done for the common good.

This brings up the idea of synergy. I would never want to underestimate the power of one person. History is replete with individuals who heroically have made a difference in the world. But there is unparalleled strength by joining strengths, by connecting creative energies, by establishing a sense of team. I once asked a group of high school students to recall a "life highlight" since they had been in high school. The answers were fascinating. One said, "I loved being in the band, especially the trips and contests." Another volunteered, "Being on the football team that won the conference championship. There was a feeling that we had worked so hard together." Still another mentioned, "For me, working on the school paper was a highlight. There is so much pressure to meet deadlines. Yet we all had fun together."

All of these students point to the fact that through organizations something gets done and done with a feeling of satisfaction. One person deciding to build a house might work for years. But an organization such as Habitat for Humanity can create a synergy of workers and complete a house in one week. Contractors help. Suppliers help. Volunteers help. Something is accomplished because a critical gathering of people is organized. As ineffectual as organizations can be, it needs to be affirmed again and again that organizations can and do make powerful differences for humanity. I can mention organizations such as Oxfam, the NAACP, the Red Cross, and the National Conference of Christians and Jews. These are all examples of people coming together and helping others in far-ranging ways that dramatically surpass the effort of one person.

I also find that organizations create lasting relationships. It is true that organizations call us beyond ourselves to care for the well-being of others. But it is equally true that in organizations we find personal and meaningful encounters with people who forever will change our lives. Because I now serve as a trustee at three different educational institutions, I have some appreciation for the complexity of organization required in a school. As a student, I was clueless. All I know is that I signed up for classes, attended classes, and eventually reached a point of graduation. But in that process of participating in an organization, I came to know professors who changed my life forever. Their love of learning impressed, inspired, and infused within me a passion of lifelong learning for myself. And in addition to faculty friendships, I became friends with classmates, people I know and continue to stay in touch with, learn from, network with from time to time. All of this happened because someone had a dream for a school, and, even more important, someone was committed enough to organize the dream.

Even now as a trustee I find myself growing closer to other trustees who give of their time and money. These are people who share in the common dream of education. I actually look forward to trustee meetings, not necessarily because I like making difficult decisions, but because I enjoy my participation in the lives of other trustees. And during those meetings I sometimes have a mystical feeling that the experience I had as a student is now being passed on to others. I don't know the students. I'm not connected to them in a personal way. But I feel as if through the structures and meetings and committees of the institution, something full and rich is being made available to them. In this sense, the students are friends; I am their traveling companion through the structures of organization.

A vital feeling comes through participation in community life. I once thanked the president of my seminary for all of his hard work and service. His response was telling. "I feel as if through the friends and relationships and experiences I have had through the years, I have gotten much more out of it than what I put in." On the one hand, he was wrong. No one worked harder than this president. Yet, on the other hand, he was right. He had experienced the miracle and mystery of participation. Yes, a touchstone.

Stories of Community

Part of my life calling is working with community. Particularly I do this with churches I have served. Churches are thick with stories and experiences, becoming interesting places to engage the many dimensions of community. They are not the only places of community. Community is both attitude and action waiting to be created in the hearts and lives of people. I have seen the shadow side of churches. I even have been on the end of inexplicable hostility and anger. Nevertheless, as I look back on a career of serving churches, I remember again and again the power of community.

One story I recall with amazing vividness took place at Southport Christian Church in Indianapolis, Indiana. Southport was and continues to be an amazing community of people. There was a spirit at Southport that was indefatigable. If we dreamed it, we assumed we could do it. People were doers. Ready to pitch in and participate in any good cause. I had to work hard just to keep up with their creativity and energy.

Someone from our denomination suggested that we could help re-settle a refugee family. This is an important ministry given the fact that there are literally millions of refugees around the world. To help them resettle and find a better life is an important contribution to global community.

Yet, issues related to refugee resettlement test the people trying to facilitate this resettlement. Some feel as if there are too many "foreigners" in our country, that somehow these people are taking prosperity away from Americans. The reality of xenophobia, fear of the stranger, is easily engaged when a group decides to participate in resettlement. Interestingly enough, the issue of culture also is raised. Do we resettle a family and then try to convert them to the Christian faith? Do we try to make Americans out of these refugees? There is also the practical responsibility that a congregation does not resettle a family overnight. This is a long-term commitment of financial and emotional support, and it strings out over several months, if not years, of transition.

After much discussion, the congregation of Southport Christian Church decided to become the sole sponsor of a family. A call came to us on a Monday morning. "We have a family for you. Vietnamese. There are seven in the family. They will arrive tomorrow night at the airport at 11:00." Wow. A couple of deep breaths were taken and a quiet prayer uttered. This was really going to happen.

I remember I went to the airport with one of our laypersons. We stood in the terminal waiting for a plane to arrive from Seattle. The best we could figure was that this family had been traveling for two straight days. No sleep. Their only food was that which was served on the airplane. A mother. A father. Five children. I will never forget seeing them for the first time. They came off that plane exhausted, hungry, and utterly bewildered. The children were beautiful. The parents barely had enough confidence to look us bright Americans in the eye. They could not speak a word of English. Not one single word. They had no luggage except for the plastic sack each of them carried. It was an incredible moment of starting over. What trust, what courage, what nerve it took for them to leave everything familiar. Seeing them walk into that terminal, I could have wept for the human poignancy of the moment.

How far they had come, but how far they still had to go. Would they find a home? Jobs? Would the kids be able to enter school? What about medical care? Dental care? What about transportation? Would they face prejudice? Would they feel cold stares and resentment because of the color of their skin or the slant of their eyes? And would the word "Vietnam" trigger old wounds and feelings in the congregation?

What I saw happening was the unfolding of community. I saw a congregation of people rise to the occasion. No, they did more than rise, they soared with the opportunity. "We have some old bedroom furniture," one family volunteered. "We have a kitchen table, only six chairs, but they're welcome to it," said another. Some would teach them how to go to the grocery. Some would enroll the children in school. Some would help them fill out applications for a job. Still others would bring the family to social events, like their first Sunday afternoon church softball game. Everyone involved was changed by this experience.

The Ngyen family is now, years later, happy, working, and educated. They bought their first house a few years ago, I understand. And the church was changed. Our concept of brother or sister was enlarged. Our appreciation for other cultures was enhanced. Our opportunity to move past our little Midwestern world, really to embrace someone different yet profoundly similar, was experienced. It was a moment of community. Could one person have done all of this? Perhaps, but highly unlikely. Instead, it was an organization, many of them in fact, and the common good was passed on like a bright candle lit in a dark room.

A second story of community is very different. This time, rather than helping a Vietnamese family, Beargrass Christian Church in Louisville, Kentucky, decided it wanted to share the gift of music. There was first of all a dream. I suggested to our director of music, Daniel Spurlock, that we create a series of pops concerts. I said, "Let's have them outdoors on a Sunday night. Turn the parking lot into an amphitheatre. Instead of doing 'church stuff,' we can do pops music. Let's give the community the gift of a night out, lots of fun, lots of music, a great big block party."

He wasn't sure what the choir would think. "Do you think a church should be doing this kind of music? We're pretty traditional around here. It won't hurt to look into it."

More conversation. More discussion. Finally a decision was made. Three outdoor pops concerts. *Beargrass Summer Sing* would be the title. We decided to invite the entire city. The first concert theme would be *Disney at Beargrass*. All the great Disney music would be sung by a one-hundred-member combined chorus. The second concert would be *Red, White, and Beargrass*—a Fourth of July event complete with fireworks. The third concert would be *Beargrass Goes to the Movies*. Great musical themes from movies would be enjoyed.

I still remember discussions in the committee meetings. "How many do you think will show up?" No one knew. I thought it would go well, but there was no guarantee. "Maybe, if we're lucky, 400 people." The first night we had more than 1,500 people come to the concert. By the end of the summer, we had hit 2,000! It was a party, a happening, a moment of pure fun and grace. And people worked hard, really hard to make it possible. Thousands of hours were volunteered. Yet one person summed it up after the last concert, "I've never worked so hard and been so exhausted, and I can't wait until next year!"

Those concerts gave the congregation a feeling of community, but they also gave the city of Louisville a feeling of community. No one could have predicted the success, but that is the way it is with community. The more we become involved, the more synergy is possible.

My third story of community is with the church I am presently serving, University Christian Church. UCC is a remarkable place because it is filled with remarkable people. I have never seen a church with so many talented and caring people as I see each week at UCC. It is hard even to describe the sense of history and hope for the future that is alive in this community, not to mention the influence it has in the city of Fort Worth.

In October 1996 a young family in our church was struck with tragedy. The man was well respected in the community and church. He was married to a lovely woman, and together they had two young children. Reed died suddenly of a heart attack on a Sunday night. They had been at church that morning. In fact, Gayla on that Sunday night had just dropped the kids off for youth group and called home on the car phone to say that she was going to stop by the video store to pick up a movie to watch. When she arrived home ten minutes later, he was dead. It is hard to overestimate the impact of this loss upon her, the children, the entire church community.

Yet, in the face of this loss, I saw the power of community. Friends waited with her in the hospital. Friends stood by the children as their hearts broke with grief. Meals were prepared, of course. But more than the typical expressions of sympathy, I have seen a church community take this family under its wings to provide love, warmth, and support. It is the power of community. In a remarkable gesture of gratitude, when we had our fall financial campaign, Gayla was the first person in the entire church to submit a pledge of support for the upcoming year.

I look at this family, and I don't really know how they are surviving. They loved each other so much. There was so much to look forward to. Their grief is beyond my comprehension. But somehow they are making it. And I know that whatever spiritual strength they find to survive is, at least in part, a strength that comes from community. In a note, Gayla recently said to me, "We have to take one day at a time, but I know we have come this far because of our friends at University Christian Church."

All three stories become a matrix for understanding community. Community is attitude. Community is action. Community is receiving. Community is giving. Community is stretching far. Community is drawing close. Community is going beyond ourselves. Community is truly finding ourselves. Community reaches out toward God. God reaches in through community. Community asks so much. Community gives so much. For many, finding genuine community may be the scariest step and most demanding touchstone. Yet, to touch and be touched by the mystery of community, to feel oneself a part of the human family is like discovering electricity for the first time. Or maybe like lighting an awaiting candle inside our soul and in the souls of others.

A Postscript

To come to an end is also to come to a beginning. And what is the beginning? For me, it is the beginning that to be alive—fully, joyfully, deliciously alive—is the most sacred calling we can answer in life. This calling moves inward and outward. Sometimes experienced in the quiet listening of prayer or in the silence of a walk through a forest. Sometimes experienced in the suffering of relationships or in the beauty of friendships. Sometimes this call is felt in music or art or drama or poetry or film. Big rituals and little rituals alike embody this call. If we will listen, deeply listen, this call to life can be heard in both work and play. The call can be heard in the flickering movement of a dog's tail that is so joyful as you walk through the door at the end of a day. The call is found in the eyes of children of every culture and every race, convincing us that there is indeed one human family.

Throughout this book I have suggested that touchstone moments are those mystical moments when ordinary life shines, if only briefly, and in that moment we forever are changed. We are changed because we have been touched by something bigger and deeper and more lovely than we ever thought possible. Some have suggested, and I agree, that we as human beings are "wired for God." It is true. It must be so. Because ultimately all longing in life is a religious longing, satisfied only by the feast that takes place upon the table of the soul.

To cherish touchstone moments requires that we both lose something and find something. What we lose is our self-consciousness, but what we find is a depth of conscious living. What we lose is our one-dimensional seeing, but what we find is complex vision and feeling. What we lose is our utter aloneness, but what we find is a depth of companionship with ourselves and God that sustains like bread and wine and cheese.

179

I invite you to live your journey. Experience is everything. Be bold. Live fully. God is that companion who is always one step ahead, calling, beckoning, luring us into the future. Dangerous? A little dangerous. But as we live, there are stones along the way. We pick them up. Hold them in our hands. We touch them against our skin. These touchstones release a kind of magic in our lives, setting something free that is within us or, viewed differently, bringing something home that never should have left.

The poet Mary Oliver asks: "Tell me, what is it you plan to do with your one wild and precious life?"[1] A haunting question? Perhaps. But for me, I hear in that question the adventure of a lifetime, the only adventure I can live, my adventure, my lifetime. And you can hear that call to live fully too. I cannot live your journey any more than you can live mine. But together we can move forward into the beauty of what it means to be me, what it means to be you, what it means to be us. And as we go, we experience the touchstones of our living and are changed forever by them.

Notes

Introduction

[1]Rainer Maria Rilke, *Selected Poems of Rainer Maria Rilke* (New York: Harper and Row, 1981), p. 13.

Chapter 1: Relationships

[1]Harville Hendrix, *Getting the Love You Want: A Guide for Couples* (New York: Henry Holt, 1988), p. 12.

[2]Mechthild of Magdeburg, quoted in *Chalice Hymnal* (St. Louis: Chalice Press, 1995), p.1.

Chapter 2: Stories

[1]Dan Wakefield, *Returning: A Spiritual Journey* (Boston: Beacon Press, 1984), p. 3.

[2]Ibid., pp. 3–4.

[3]Ibid., pp. 27–28.

[4]Eric Clapton, *Tears in Heaven* (Burbank, Calif.: Reprise Records, 1991).

[5]Source untraced.

[6]Toni Morrison, *Beloved* (New York: Alfred E. Knopf, 1987), pp. 87–88.

Chapter 3: Rituals

[1]Louis Charpentier, *The Mysteries of Chartres Cathedral*, trans. Ronald Fraser (New York: Gallery Books, W. H. Smith, 1985), p. 68.

[2]Lee G. Bolman and Terrence E. Deal, *Leading with Soul: An Uncommon Journey of Spirit* (San Francisco: Jossey Bass, 1995), p. 111.

[3]Robert Fulghum, *From Beginning to End: The Rituals of Our Lives* (New York: Villard Books, 1995), p. 21.

[4]Terrence E. Deal and Allen A. Kennedy, *Corporate Cultures: The Rites and Rituals of Corporate Life* (Reading, Mass.: Addison-Wesley Publishing, 1984), p. 61.

Chapter 4: Art

[1]Frank L. Kernowski and Alice Hughes, *Conversations with Henry Miller* (Jackson: University Press of Mississippi, 1994), p. 153.

[2]Julie Cameron, *The Artist's Way* (New York: G. P. Putnam's Sons, 1992), p. 7.

[3]Matthew Fox, *The Coming of the Cosmic Christ* (San Francisco: Harper and Collins, 1988), p. 58.

[4]Ibid., pp. 58–59.

[5]William Carlos Williams, *Selected Poems* (New York: New Directions, 1985), p. 56.

[6]Robert Bly, *The Kabir Book: Forty-four of the Ecstatic Poems of Kabir* (Boston: Beacon Press, 1971), p. 214.

Chapter 5: Prayer

[1]James Hillman, *Insearch: Psychology and Religion*(New York.: Charles Scribner's Sons, 1967), p. 21.

[2]William Butler Yeats, *Selected Poems and Three Plays of William Butler Yeats* (New York: MacMillan Publishing, 1986), pp. 141–42.

[3]Thich Nhat Hanh, *Living Buddha, Living Christ* (New York: G.P. Putran's Sons, 1995), p. 14.

[4]Hayden Carruth, *Scrambled Eggs and Whiskey: Poems 1991–1995* (Port Townsend, Wash.: Copper Canyon Press, 1996), p. 11.

[5]Source untraced

[6]Cornell West, *Race Matters* (Boston: Beacon Press, 1993), p. 1.

[7]Thich Nhat Hanh, p. 87.

[8]Antonio Machado, *Selected Poems* (Cambridge, Mass.: Harvard University Press, 1982), p. 93.

[9]David Steindl-Rast, *The Music of Silence* (San Francisco: Harper Collins, 1995), p. 29.

Chapter 6: Play and Work

[1]Donald Hall, *Life Work* (Boston: Beacon Press, 1993), p. 8.

[2]George Leonard, *The Ultimate Athlete: Re-Visioning Sports, Physical Education and the Body* (Berkeley, Calif.: North Atlantic Books, 1990), p. 61.

[3]Mihaly Csikszentmihalyi, *Flow: The psychology of Optimal Experience* (San Francisco: Harper Collins, 1991), p. 3.

[4]Fred Shoemaker, *Extraordinary Golf: The Art of the Possible* (New York: G. P. Putnam's Sons, 1996), p. 11.

[5]George Plimpton, *The X Factor: A Quest for Excellence* (New York: Norton and Co., 1995), p. 7.

[6]Dorothy Bass, *Practicing Our Faith: A Way of Life for Searching People* (San Francisco: Jossey-Bass, 1997, p. 89.

Chapter 7: Nature

[1]Annie Dillard, *Holy the Firm* (New York: Harper and Row, 1977), p. 11.

[2]Ibid., p. 30.

[3]Robert Bly, *News of the Universe: Poems of Twofold Consciousness* (San Francisco: Sierra Club Books, 1980), p. 173.

[4]Source untraced.

A Postscript

[1]Mary Oliver, *House of Light* (Boston: Beacon Press, 1990), p. 60.